Louis Sachar

Holes

Teacher's Guide
with copymasters

Mechthild Hesse
Miriam Bögel

Ernst Klett Sprachen
Stuttgart

Herausgegeben von Mechthild Hesse und Miriam Bögel
unter Mitarbeit von Hannelore Born, Dorothea Ernst,
Ursula Hebel-Zipper, Annegret Kossak, Maria Jungels,
Anne Zenk.

Table of contents

Introduction   3
1.1   The novel   3
1.1.1   Short summary   3
1.1.2   Structure and chapter summaries   4

2.   Teaching the novel   6
2.1   The relationship between speaking, reading and writing   6
2.2   Overview of the teaching unit   8
2.3   How to get into the novel: Reading strategies   9

3.   Worksheets – solutions   10

4.   Further assignments and mini projects   29

5.   Assessment   29

6.   The film   29
6.1   Overview   30
6.2   Viewing tasks   33

7.   Additional materials   35

8.   Bibliography   35

9.   Useful URLs   35

Worksheets   36

Film terminology (copymaster)   59

Student self-assessment   60

2. Auflage   2 ⁵ ⁴ ³ | 2015 14 13

Redaktion: Dr. Hartmut K. Selke

Grafik Seite 59: Christian Dekelver, Weinstadt
Titelbild: Cinetext GmbH, Frankfurt
Druck und Bindung: Digitaldruck Tebben, Biessenhofen
Printed in Germany

ISBN 978-3-12-578171-9

1. Introduction

This teacher's book is both an attempt to make reading a novel an in-class experience and at the same time to improve the students' language skills. The idea is that classroom talk should be prepared by or lead to students' writing. For this reason the workbook offers a wide variety of writing tasks and helps students how to fulfill these tasks.

How to use this guide

The first part of this teacher's guide is meant to be read only by teachers.

Chapters 1 and 2 contain a plot summary and teaching. Glances at the plot survey and the teaching overviews will help teachers to quickly retrieve specific information, which will help them to save time.

Chapter 3 offers possible solutions for the worksheets, except those which call for creative artwork on the part of the students (e.g. creating an advertisement, drawing pictures, etc.). For other creative, imaginary texts we have chosen one solution and printed it here, which, however, obviously does not mean that this is the only possible solution. Texts, however, which "only" retrieve information from the novel are meant as model solutions.

Chapter 4 contains the worksheets. For most worksheets we have tried to find interesting tasks that help students understand the novel by closely looking at the text and creating their own images. Some assignments may only be used in advanced classes (11th grade and up), some are also usable in 9th and 10th grade classes. The novel itself, we believe, can be read from grade 9 on. Of course certain challenging tasks should be omitted, though they may later be used in other contexts. We want to show here that the novel gives rise to a great variety of assignments. In any case, we suggest that only a selection of these writing assignments be used in any one class, as too many writing assignments might lessen the reading enjoyment that the book offers.

Chapter 5 to 8 is a mixture of information for teachers and students, suggestions for teachers, worksheets (assessment) and additional materials. You will need to decide which information you want to give to your students and which to keep to yourself.

1.1 The novel

Holes won the most prestigious U.S. children's book award, the Newbery Medal in 1999 and was short-listed for other international prizes. Holes is an exciting story that combines realistic, historical, fantastic and humorous elements, which should be fun and informative material for lively classroom discussions. The movie with Shia LaBeouf as Stanley was also a great success.

1.1.1 Short summary

Ever since a one-legged gypsy put a curse on his great-great-grandfather, the male members of Stanley Yelnats's family have been suffering from bad luck. They tend to be in the wrong place at the wrong time. Consequently, young Stanley gets unjustly sent to a boot camp for boys, Camp Green Lake in the Texan desert. He is charged with having stolen the valuable sneakers of the famous baseball star Clyde Livingston, but in fact he was hit by the shoes falling from a bridge.

When Stanley arrives at Camp Green Lake, he sees that there is no lake, only a desert-like landscape in which the boys have to dig a hole five feet wide and five feet deep every day, supposedly a character building measure. Soon Stanley realizes that the camp's female warden is really using the boys to look for something valuable, the hidden treasure of Kissin' Kate Barlow, the famous Western outlaw.

In the camp Stanley makes friends with Hector Zeroni, called Zero. They make a deal that Stanley teaches Zero to read and Zero, in return, digs part of Stanley's hole for him every day. Their friendship intensifies when, one after the other, they flee from the camp. With a little bit of luck and with the help of their own newly acquired skills, they survive in the desert, and on sneaking back to the camp they really find the treasure that the warden has been looking for all her life. The luck becomes complete when Stanley's parents, who so far have been too poor to afford a lawyer, find one who frees both Stanley and Zero from the camp and takes them home. When both families' common roots are discovered, the spell is finally broken.

1.1.2 Structure and chapter summaries

Part 1: You Are Entering Camp Green Lake

Chapter 1: The camp – its location, its rules, its dangers – is introduced in an ironic way.

Chapter 2: The camp is presented as a camp for "bad boys". Stanley, however, is not a bad, but only a poor boy who has been sent there by the judge.

Chapter 3: It becomes clear to the reader that Stanley is innocent of the crime he has been charged with. He blames his arrest on the streak of bad luck that runs in his family starting with his Latvian pig-stealing great-great grandfather, who immigrated to the USA and was plagued by bad luck.

Chapter 4: After a 9-hour bus ride Stanley is welcomed by the guard, Mr. Sir, who explains the basic rules and the dangers of the camp. We learn that Stanley will have to stay at the camp for 18 months.

Chapter 5: The boys' tent is described in detail. Armpit gets angry when he is called by his real name, Theodore.

Chapter 6: The reader learns about Stanley's "crime". He was arrested for holding on to shoes which had dropped onto his head from a bridge.

Chapter 7: On the first day of digging holes at the camp, Stanley is told to report everything unusual he might find in the ground.

The story of his great-great-grandfather in Latvia is told: After having been refused as a wedding candidate by the father of his love Myra, he gets help from Madame Zeroni. By carrying a piglet up a mountain where the water is said to run uphill, he and his pig get so strong that he is finally able to compete with the other candidate, who is rich and has a fat pig. When the pigs of both candidates weigh the same and the girl still cannot decide whom to marry, he realizes that he wooed the wrong girl and leaves her and Latvia in order to go to America.

On the day he leaves he realizes that he has forgotten to carry Madame Zeroni uphill, too, a promise he had made to her when he asked her for help in his love affair with the girl. After several incidents of bad luck in America, this broken promise leads him to believe that there is a curse on him.

At the end of the day Stanley is proud of his work as a hole digger.

Chapter 8: The danger to life posed by the yellow spotted lizards is explained in detail.

Chapter 9: Without knowing it, Stanley – like the other inmates – has been given a nickname, Caveman, which shows that he is accepted as part of the group. Stanley writes his first letter to his mother.

Chapter 10: On the second day of digging Stanley turns in a fossil he has found. He learns, however, that fossils are of no interest to the Warden or the camp guards.

Chapter 11: Stanley meditates about the ranking in the group and is surprised at being accepted so quickly, which had never been the case at school.

Chapter 12: In a counseling session with Mr Pendanski the boys are asked to think about their crimes and to make plans for their future after the camp. When Stanley seriously blames his great-great grandfather for his bad luck, the boys, and among them especially Zero, are amused.

Chapter 13: Stanley finds a gold tube in the ground, shows it to the group, and X-Ray decides to keep it for himself so that he might get a day off. Stanley even helps him to take advantage of it. After that Stanley moves up in the camp's hierarchy.

Chapter 14: The following morning X-Ray presents the tube and promptly gets a day off. The Warden appears for the first time and shows her absolute authority over inmates and guards alike.

Chapter 15: The boys realize that building character is not the predominant goal of digging: that day all the three wardens watch the boys, who know now that they are obviously looking for something specific. Zigzag claims that the boys are constantly observed by tiny cameras and their voices heard over microphones.

Chapter 16: The find has triggered the interest of the warden so much that she wants the boys to dig more thoroughly. Stanley receives another letter from his mother, which makes him laugh. Zero cannot understand Stanley's reaction, not even after Stanley explains the pun, because he does not know the nursery rhyme "There was an old lady who lived in a shoe".

Chapter 17: The Warden has become so excited over the find that she has even started digging herself. Zigzag's shovel hits Stanley and the boys fight over whose dirt it is they are shoveling.

Chapter 18: When their search proves futile, they start digging at another site. When Stanley writes a letter to his mom, Zero asks him to teach him to read.

Chapter 19: Mr. Sir who is distributing water, does not realize that his sack of sunflower seeds was stolen by Magnet, who throws it around so that it lands in Stanley's hole. Stanley is taken to the Warden for punishment. This again is a sign for Stanley that he is in the wrong place at the wrong time.

Chapter 20: Stanley witnesses how the Warden punishes Mr. Sir by scratching her venomous rattlesnake nail polish into the guard's face.

Chapter 21: When Stanley comes back, his hole is almost finished. On his way back from the Warden's cabin he encounters a rattlesnake that gives a rattling warning. He remembers the story of his great-grandfather who was rescued after 17 days in the desert by rattlesnake hunters. He remembers his ancestor saying that he found refuge on "God's thumb".

Chapter 22: Stanley makes a deal with Zero: he helps him learn to read and in return Zero helps him dig. At night he realizes that the gold tube he has found is one half of a lipstick container. Thinking about the initials on the tube, it occurs to him that they stand for Kate Barlow, the "kissin' outlaw".

Chapter 23: The century-old story of Katherine Barlow is told: She was the pretty teacher of the town of Green Lake, a thriving community on the lake. She turned down Trout Walker, a member of the richest family in town, and thus hurt his feelings.

Chapter 24: Stanley is punished by Mr. Sir for the humiliation he suffered at the Warden's office: Every time Mr. Sir distributes water, he spills the water meant for Stanley on the ground.

Chapter 25: Instead of with Trout Walker, Katherine Barlow falls in love with the black onion seller and ointment mixer Sam, who proves to be a kind and helpful supporter of Katherine's school. One of the citizens sees Sam kiss Katherine.

Chapter 26: Sam becomes the victim of the ensuing lynching carried out by the white community. A few days later Kate shoots the sheriff and becomes a famous, feared outlaw. After the lynching until the present not one drop of rain has fallen on Green Lake.

Chapter 27: In spite of his thirst Stanley does not drink from his canteen because he is afraid that Mr. Sir might have added poison to the water. Zero learns to write his name and tells Stanley his real name: Hector Zeroni.

Chapter 28: After twenty years of being an outlaw and robber, Kate Barlow returns to Green Lake, where she hides in an abandoned cabin. One day Trout Walker and his wife, a former student of Kate's, walk in on her and demand to know where she is keeping her treasure. They torture her but she refuses to give in. She is finally bitten by a yellow-spotted lizard and killed immediately.

Part 2 The Last Hole

Chapter 29: The weather has changed from dry to humid heat with many thunderstorms. The mountain Big Thumb is now clearly visible. Stanley thinks of his family history and wonders how his great-grandfather might have survived in the desert without food or drink.

Chapter 30: On July 8 (if that's the date Zigzag thinks it is) Zero disappears after he is taunted by the group and the guards about being too stupid to read and write. He hits Mr. Pendanski with his shovel and disappears. The group now has to dig 7 holes with 6 people.

Chapter 31: Zero does not reappear. The Warden has Zero's file deleted from the computer assuming that he will just be forgotten, because he has no family and is a ward of the state.

Chapter 32: Twitch arrives to take Zero's place. Stanley decides to go after Zero to find him. As he thinks he needs a car to catch up with him, he steals Mr. Sir's truck, but he drives the truck into one of the holes the boys have dug and has to continue his search on foot.

Chapter 33: Stanley heads in the direction of Big Thumb. He looks into each hole to see if Zero is hiding there, but he cannot find him. In one of the holes he discovers a family of yellow-spotted lizards and runs away.

Chapter 34: He sets off to examine an object he sees in the far distance. The object turns out to be part of a boat turned upside down with Mary Lou written on it in faded letters. Zero, who had found shelter underneath the wreck, crawls out from under it.

Chapter 35: Both have "sploosh", preserved peaches from a glass jar, which they estimate to be about 100 years old. Zero is not willing to go back to the camp and refuses to listen to Stanley's plan. Zero has stomach cramps, probably from eating too much "sploosh". The mountain he sees in front of him reminds Stanley of his ancestor's tales about Big Thumb.

Chapter 36: After walking through the plain of the dried lake they arrive at the western rim, which is shaped like a cliff. With all his ingenuity Stanley helps Zero to climb over the rim and both walk up in the shade of Big Thumb.

Chapter 37: While climbing, they notice weeds and bugs, signs of water.

Chapter 38: Stanley, who is carrying Zero, falls into a muddy hole from which he licks water. Digging deeper he finds an onion, which he shares with Zero.

Chapter 39: Stanley tries to decide whether he should go back to pick up the shovel, which he had left behind when he carried Zero up the hill. Zero makes a confession: it was he who stole Clyde Livingston's sneakers.

Chapter 40: In a flashback we learn about Sam, the onion seller, who used to cure all kinds of illnesses with onions in the community of Green Lake. Stanley and Zero live on onions,

and gradually Zero's condition improves. Stanley walks down the mountain to look for the shovel. He finds it way down and has to make the strenuous climb back up again.

Chapter 41: Zero tells Stanley about his life as a street kid. He was used to stealing food and other things necessary to survive.

Chapter 42: Stanley is happy. He has a friend and has a plan: he wants to find Kate Barlow's treasure.

Chapter 43: Zero tells Stanley about his experiences before and after his family became homeless. Stanley confesses that his family, too, may be confronted with homelessness as they may be evicted from their home. Talking about common experiences, they go back to the camp, where they hide in the hole in which Stanley had found the golden tube.

Chapter 44: Zero goes off to steal some food from the camp kitchen. The two boys take turns digging. Finally Stanley hits a metal suitcase. The moment they finally manage to pry the suitcase free, the Warden's voice is heard thanking them for finding the treasure for her.

Chapter 45: In the hole Stanley realizes he is standing in a nest of yellow-spotted lizards and the Warden waits for them to give him the final bite so that she can take possession of the suitcase. We learn that the Warden is the daughter of Trout Walker, who apparently had spent the rest of his life digging for Kate Barlow's treasure.

Chapter 46: The Warden and the guards talk about how they will tell Stanley's mother and the Attorney General that Stanley ran away, fell into a hole and was killed by the lizards. The lizards, however, just crawl over Stanley, but do not bite him.

Chapter 47: The boys are still scared of the many lizards in the hole, when a lawyer appears who wants to file charges against the camp for child abuse. The lawyer has a court order demanding the release of Stanley. The Warden claims that Stanley stole the suitcase from her own cabin. The boys slowly creep out of the hole with the suitcase, which, to everybody's surprise, has STANLEY YELNATS written on it.

Chapter 48: Stanley is released due to an order from the judge. As Zero's file cannot be found, Zero is also released.

Chapter 49: In a flashback we learn that Sam, the onion seller, sold pure onion juice as a protection against lizard bites. The yellow-spotted lizards, we are told, don't like onion blood. Stanley and Zero are in the lawyer's, Ms. Morengo's, BMW on the way back home. Ms. Morengo, who is Stanley's father's patent attorney, tells that Stanley's father has invented something that eliminates foot odor.

Part 3 Filling in the Holes

Chapter 50: Camp Green Lake has to be closed and will later be opened as a camp for girl scouts.

Stanley's father forces open the suitcase and finds not jewelry, but also valuable stock certificates that make Stanley and Zero millionaires. The money enables them to hire private investigators to find Zero's mother.

At a party at the Yelnats' house, Clyde Livingston, who is one of the guests, watches himself in a TV advertisement for the new foot odor cure Stanley's father has invented.

The last words of the novel are the words of the "if only" song sung by a woman who is fluffing Zero's hair. Who may this woman be? This is a hole the readers have to fill in themselves.

2. Teaching the novel

2.1 The relationship between speaking, reading and writing

This teacher's guide is not one that suggests ideas for each individual lesson. It centers around the idea of improving the students' reading and writing skills, skills that – as PISA shows – require much practice. This teacher's guide aims to avoid the danger of "discussing literature to death". We want to point out that reading is first of all an individual activity that, especially for non-native speakers, must be taught. It means that **reading strategies** have to be acquired in order to make it possible for students to read long texts, maybe several chapters at a time, at home and in the classroom. Thus we will first deal with reading strategies which (as the PISA study clearly showed) learners need to be able to understand in order to work with the text.

We are strongly convinced that reading, however, needs the support of writing and that writing is the best way to make sure that firstly each reader has understood the text and secondly that he/she really can respond individually to the text, as the response theory postulates. Therefore, the teacher's guide takes the form of a workbook with worksheets for teachers to copy and use in class. A variety of text forms has been included in an attempt to provide more comprehensive examples of the types of writing that students must master in order to pass exams and move on to the following grades. High-quality writing should be expected, but it should also be carefully prepared for and taught in advance.

The writing process

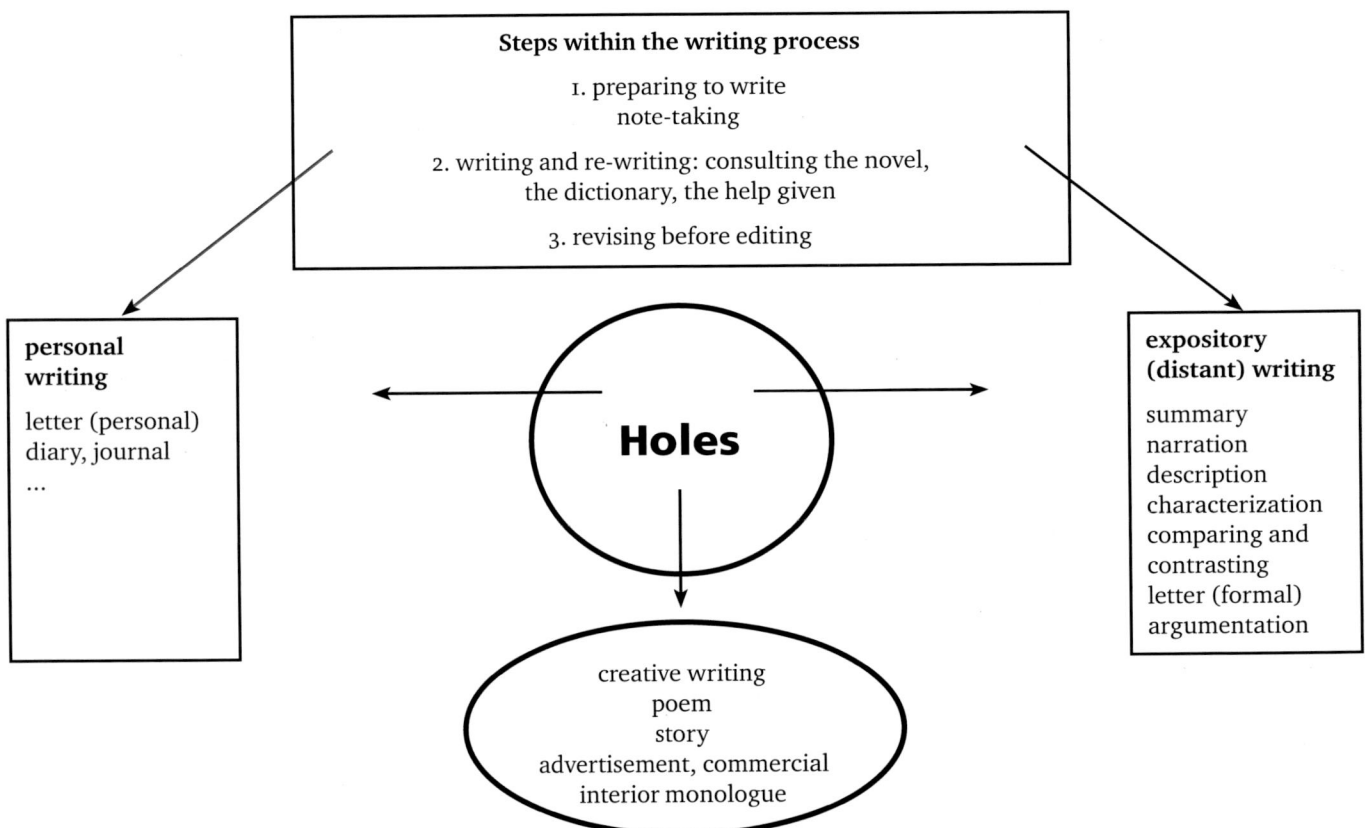

Steps within the writing process

1. preparing to write
   note-taking

2. writing and re-writing: consulting the novel, the dictionary, the help given

3. revising before editing

personal writing

letter (personal)
diary, journal
...

Holes

expository (distant) writing

summary
narration
description
characterization
comparing and contrasting
letter (formal)
argumentation

creative writing
poem
story
advertisement, commercial
interior monologue

When writing the students should take three things into consideration: the addressee and purpose of the text, what vocabulary is necessary and appropriate to both addressee and purpose, and what organizing rules should be applied. Thinking about these three matters should help learners to weave specific information from the novel into their own writing and thus expand their own vocabulary and skill at writing fully developed paragraphs and multi-paragraph papers. Assessing student writing will become easier when criteria are developed and clarified before the writing takes place.

In our model papers (teacher's solutions) we included difficult vocabulary and wrote texts for more advanced students.

However, most of these assignments can also be done in 9th and 10th grade classes where less complex texts could be the outcome.

All the texts are aimed at helping students to improve their writing. Some are just preparations for writing (note-taking exercises), some are good for personal writing (letter, diary, etc.), others can be used in academic writing and for the development of analytical abilities (characterization, summary, review, etc.); and yet others again can be used for personal creative responses (poem, story, advertisement, etc.). Teachers are asked to select materials and assignments depending on the class in which *Holes* is read.

Text types used in this guide

Preparatory writing	Personal writing	Expository writing	Creative writing
Note-taking: Stanley's Profile (W 1) Crossword Puzzle (W2) Family tree (W 5) The beginning of a friendship: Stanley and Zero (W 8) Description of the camp (W 4) and the guards (W 12) Film: Bootcamp (W 20) **Connecting sentences:** Kate Barlow's Story (W 10) **Filling in forms:** Stanley's crime (W5) character files (W 6) Wanted poster (W 11) **Advertisement:** Camp Green Lake (W 14) Sploosh commercial (W 17)	**Personal letter:** letter to Stanley's mother (W 9) **Formal letter:** letter to the Attorney General (W 13) **Report:** steps to friendship (W 18)	**Summary:** film and book review (W 21) **Narration:** Stanley's crime (W 5) **Historical narration:** Kate Barlow (W 10) **Analytical description:** steps to friendship (W 18) **Description of the camp** (W 4) **Characterization:** character files (W 6) Character relationships (W 7) **Comparison and contrast:** film and reality (W 19) **Formal letter:** letter to the Attorney General (W 13) **Argumentation:** panel discussion (W 21) **Comparison and contrast** essay: the guards (W 20)	**Story** of Stanley's crime (W 3) **Interior monologue:** Stanley's new sense of self (W 15) **Poem/song:** "If only" (W 19) **Advertisement:** Camp Green Lake (W 14) **TV script** for a Sploosh commercial (W 17) **Interview** with Stanley's father (W 16) Wanted **poster** (W 11)

What the texts will all have in common is that Holes as a literary text is used as their basis. Our aims should be to teach students how to appreciate this novel in its own right and to help students improve their knowledge of English and their writing skills.

This does not mean, however, that the classroom should become only a writing laboratory.

Writing has to be introduced, prepared and followed by class discussions in which ideas are shared and different reactions to the novel can be voiced. We have to be aware of the fact (and maybe explain this to students) that the classroom is a precious place for students where their individual responses to the literary text can be discussed, checked, listened to, supported, argued against, in short, where they can effectively communicate with other readers.

Individual responses to literary texts often involve questions of identity, which makes the literary classroom an important element in adolescents' lives. Teachers and students alike have to be aware that students later in life will seldom have the chance to be able to exchange their ideas so intensely. We are trying to provide a classroom that not only tests and raises comprehension questions which can easily be answered by "right or wrong", but that also provides tasks which give room to students' individuality, creativity and search for identity.

2.2 Overview of the teaching unit

Although the author divided the novel into three parts (as part of his humorous design), the teaching of *Holes* should consist of five parts or units. This division seems necessary as the story line consists of five separate sections.

The headings for the five parts can be found in the table of contents and in the left column of the table below. Test papers can be written at any point in the reading process (cf. assessment chapter).

section	content	assignments
Part 1 **Chapters 1–8** **Introducing the camp, its rules and the characters**	Getting into the novel the camp Stanley, as a new inmate, sees the camp Stanley's file reason for Stanley's arrest: his "crime" from his point of view Stanley's past/ the curse on his family	chapters 1–3: Stanley's profile (W 1) **note-taking**: nicknames, crossword puzzle (W 2) chapters 4–5 **diary entry**: Description of the camp from Stanley's point of view (W 3) chapters 3 and 6: note-taking: **filling in a form:** Stanley's crime **narration**: Stanley's crime (W 4) after chapter 7: **note-taking**: family tree (W 5)
Part 2 **Chapters 9–22** **Digging, searching, finding: Life in the camp**	the camp inmates the beginning of a friendship: Stanley and Zero first hints at treasure	after chapter 9: **note-taking**: character files (W 6) **character** relationships (W 7) from chapter 12 onwards: **note-taking**: The beginning of a friendship: Stanley and Zero (worksheet to accompany the reading process: W 8) **letter writing**: Stanley writes a letter to his mother inquiring about the K.B. lipstick lid (W 9)
Part 3 **Chapters 23–28** **The mystery unfolds: Past and present getting closer**	Kate Barlow	Chapters 23, 25, 26 and 28: **historical narration**: Kate Barlow's story (W 10) **note-taking and poster**: Kate Barlow wanted poster (W 11)
Part 4 **Chapters 29–39** **Heading for a solution and for Big Thumb**	the camp guards the owners of the camp design an advertisement	after chapter 31: **note-taking**: description of the guards **formal letter** to the Attorney General (W 12) after chapter 32: advertisement brochure (W 13)
Part 5 **Chapters 40–50** **Catching up on the past Justice and final success**	Stanley's development Stanley's father's success story advertising "Sploosh" on TV *Holes* as a story of friendship understanding the frequently repeated song (motif?) "If only, if only"	after chapter 41: **interior monologue**: Stanley's new sense of self (W 14) **interview** with Stanley's father, the inventor of foot odor spray (W 15) Before reading chapter 50: **TV script** for a "Sploosh" commercial (W 16) **Story**: Zero tells his mother about the development of his friendship (W 17) after reading chapter 50: **creative writing: poem/ song**: "If only" (W 18)
Post-reading	boot camps in reality and this fictional boot camp panel discussion	**note-taking**: bootcamp (W 19) comparison and contrast of the guards in the film and in the book (W 20) **argumentation**: panel discussion: How effective are boot camps? (W 21) test paper

2.3 How to get into the novel: Reading strategies

PISA study experts consider the ability of using reading strategies as one variable that can well be influenced and trained so that students can learn to read and understand more complex texts with practice.

The following reading strategies have been identified among others: predicting, finding key words, making inferences from headings, etc. One main strategy is the ability to understand words that one has not come across previously, i.e. guesswork plays an important part. Thus words may be guessed from the knowledge of other words with the same root, from other languages, from the sound of the words and last but not least from the immediate or larger context. In order to practice these reading skills it is advisable to read the first three chapters together in class and to point the students in the right direction.

Step 1: Guessing – predicting from the book cover

A most obvious and successful method to make students start guessing what the book is about is examining the book cover. The holes, the dry sand, the mountains and the dark blue sky may be used to trigger ideas of what the story might be about. The original cover could also be presented which shows half of a boy's face (hinting at the irony of the story) with an orange cap and a spade. Students should write their first responses to the cover, an invented story line and their expectations on a sheet of paper that is collected and maybe hung up in the classroom, where it can be referred to at a later point.

The blurb should only be used if most of the story is not revealed in it. Of course once the book is in the students' hands, one cannot prevent them from reading and making inferences from the text. *ho – re – sitters in class*

Step 2: Guessing – on the basis of the first sentence

The heading of part one of the novel is: "You are entering Camp Green Lake." This prepares the readers for what they will discover in the next chapter. The key word "camp" should trigger student reactions, especially since even in Germany more and more sports camps that they might attend themselves in their holidays have been founded. Of course other connotations of the word "camp" will be mentioned (relating to camping or the Nazi concentration camps, for example). This brainstorming activity should prepare the students to "enter Camp Green Lake".

Step 3: Collecting bits and pieces that have been understood

The teacher reads the first two chapters aloud. (Alternatively these chapters could be presented from the audio cassette.) The students are asked to focus on what they understand and not on what they do not understand (**especially not on unknown vocabulary**). After this first reading students say **what they did understand**. What is mentioned correctly by several students should be written on the board. Thus the students' general understanding of the first chapter is positively underlined. From the notes on the board the students might form a short one-sentence summary:

"Stanley, who is from a poor family, is sent by a judge to Camp Green Lake, which is located in a dry, hot, flat wasteland far away from any human settlement but inhabited by scorpions and rattlesnakes."

Step 4: Scanning

The teacher reads chapter 3 aloud (or again, alternatively, the cassette recording is used).

This chapter is more difficult as there is a good deal of specific information given that is needed to understand Stanley's family history. As this is an important part of his biography, the reading process should be halted at this point and students should use the scanning method to retrieve specific information necessary to fill in this form (cf. teacher's solutions W1).

Step 5: Understanding unknown vocabulary

Many students at first feel uncomfortable when reading long texts; therefore word recognition strategies should be practiced in class so that students feel well prepared when left to read alone. There are four areas from which students may infer meaning: word family, other languages, context and sound. Here are a few examples from chapter 1, that can be followed by numerous other examples:

Chapter 1 p. 1

word family

dry – dried up ⇨ to dry ⇨ dryer
to own ⇨ owner

other languages
scorpion
camper

context
hammock ⇨ a hammock is **stretched between two trees**…;
campers are forbidden to **lie in** a hammock

sound
rattlesnake ⇨ snake that makes a rattling sound
(one could bring a baby rattle to class)

3. Worksheets – solutions

3.1 While-reading worksheets

W 1 Stanley's profile

Scan chapter 3 one more time and fill in the information you get
(later empty spaces can be filled in)

	Stanley	Stanley's father	Stanley's great-grandfather	Stanley's great-great-grandfather
full name	Stanley Yelnats IV	Stanley Yelnats III	Stanley Yelnats	Elya Yelnats "no-good-dirty-rotten-pig-stealing-great-great grandfather"
unusual quality of the name	spelled the same way forward and backward	spelled the same way forward and backward	spelled the same way forward and backward	
place of residence (place where he lives)	lives with his parents in a tiny apartment in California	lives with his family in a tiny apartment in California	moved from New York to California	Latvia, then emigrates to America
social conditions	rather poor;	rather poor no money for summer camp for his son	made a fortune in the stock market; lost his entire fortune when robbed by outlaw Kate Barlow	quite poor
approximate age	fifteen (?)			fifteen years when he fell in love
outward appearance (weight)	overweight			
profession / job	high school student	inventor (tries to recycle old shoes)	played the stock market	farmer
character traits	good kid; innocent of the crime; unable to defend himself when bullied	sings to his son; is smart, persevering; learns from failure		bad luck followed him
friends	none			
pastime activities	playing with stuffed animals			

NB: We learn nothing about Stanley's grandfather, but his name must obviously have been Stanley Yelnats II.

W 2 Crossword puzzle

		Y	E	L	N	A	T	S		
4	B	L	A	C	K	5	R	E	X	B
6	L				7				R	A
B	A	R	F	8	Z	I	G	Z	A	G
I	C	9			E	10	M		Y	11
G	K	Z		12	R	13	A	L	A	N
14	H	E	C	T	O	R	G		R	I
S	I	R	15	H	N	16	N		M	C
17	M	O	M	E	I	L	E		P	K
		18	J	O	S	E	T		I	
19	M	R		D	20	W	H	I	T	E
21	Z	E	R	O	R	I	C	K	Y	22
			R	23	S	Q	U	I	D	
24	C	A	V	E	M	A	N			

W 3 Diary entry: Description of the camp from Stanley's point of view

Daily routine:
This first day at the camp was like a nightmare. I am miserable. We have to dig a hole a day, five feet deep and five feet wide. The sun is blazing and it is terribly hot, but we have only one canteen of water that is filled up once a day.

Clothes:
But let me start at the beginning: when I first arrived I had to remove all my clothes and I was given a new set of camp clothes. Each set of clothes consists of an orange long-sleeve jumpsuit, an orange T-shirt, and yellow socks. Fresh laundry is provided every three days.

His tent and the camp's inmates:
Then I was shown to my smelly, scratchy cot, which another guy had just left. Like all the guys he has a nickname. His is Barf Bag. I wonder why they called him that. I also wonder why all the other guys want to be called by their nicknames, one of which is Armpit. Ugh, I guess he doesn't smell too good.

Condition of camp and counselor:
The whole camp is run down. It consists of six large gray tents lettered A to F. F is the counselors' tent. I was assigned to tent D with Mr. Pendanski as my counselor. He is younger than Mr. Sir and doesn't look as scary as Mr. Sir does.

Location within Texas:
The camp itself is located in the vast wasteland of the Texan desert. It's a desolate place. It doesn't need a fence for the next settlement is almost a nine-hour bus ride away and there is no water supply anywhere near so that the fugitives would die of thirst.

Work:
The earth is terribly hard so that my hands ache, my whole body aches, but after finally finishing my first hole I felt good.

W 4 Stanley's crime

Step 1 Stanley's criminal record

Name	Stanley Yelnats
Age	13
Place of residence	California
Crime	stole a pair of shoes from display at the homeless shelter, which famous baseball player Clyde Livingston had donated to the shelter. Auction and autograph signing would have brought at least 5,000 dollars.
Criminal record	first criminal offense
Sentence	18 months of detention
Sent to	Camp Green Lake, Texas

Step 2

That day Mrs. Bell had **made fun of** me for the umpteenth time. She used me, the heaviest kid in class, to teach us **ratios**, saying I weighed three times as much as another kid. **The worst thing** is she doesn't even realize what she's doing. And then the **bully** Derrick **tormented** me again, although he is really much smaller than I am. He stole my **notebook** and when I tried to **retrieve** it, he **dumped** it in the **toilet bowl** in the boys' bathroom. By the time I fished it out of the bowl, the bus had gone so I had to walk home. **Exactly while** I was thinking about having to copy the wet pages and **cursing** Derrick, exactly when I was walking under the bridge of the freeway overpass, these stinking shoes fell from the sky and hit me right on the head. Somebody must have really had **a bad case of foot odor** here!

Anyway, I saw this **incident** as **a sign from** God and of **destiny** – all my family **believe in fate** and most of it we **blame on** my no-good-dirty-rotten-pig-stealing-great-great-grandfather. I took the shoes with me.

I was running home quickly to give the shoes to my dad, who is trying to discover a way of recycling old sneakers, when a **patrol car** stopped next to me and I was **arrested**. I was handcuffed and put into the police car for **questioning**. I didn't understand a thing of what they were talking about and the police took a long time to tell me their story: the shoes had not **dropped from** the sky, but were the shoes of the famous **baseball star** Clyde Livingston. He had **donated** them to our local **homeless shelter**, which was going to invite famous people to have the "homeless dinner", with Clyde being there to **sign autographs**. The sneakers were to be auctioned and the organizers expected **to raise** at least five or six thousand bucks.

Once again I was in the wrong place at the wrong time like many of my ancestors had been. It was just another example of **bad luck** that seems **to be running in the family**.

W 5 Family tree

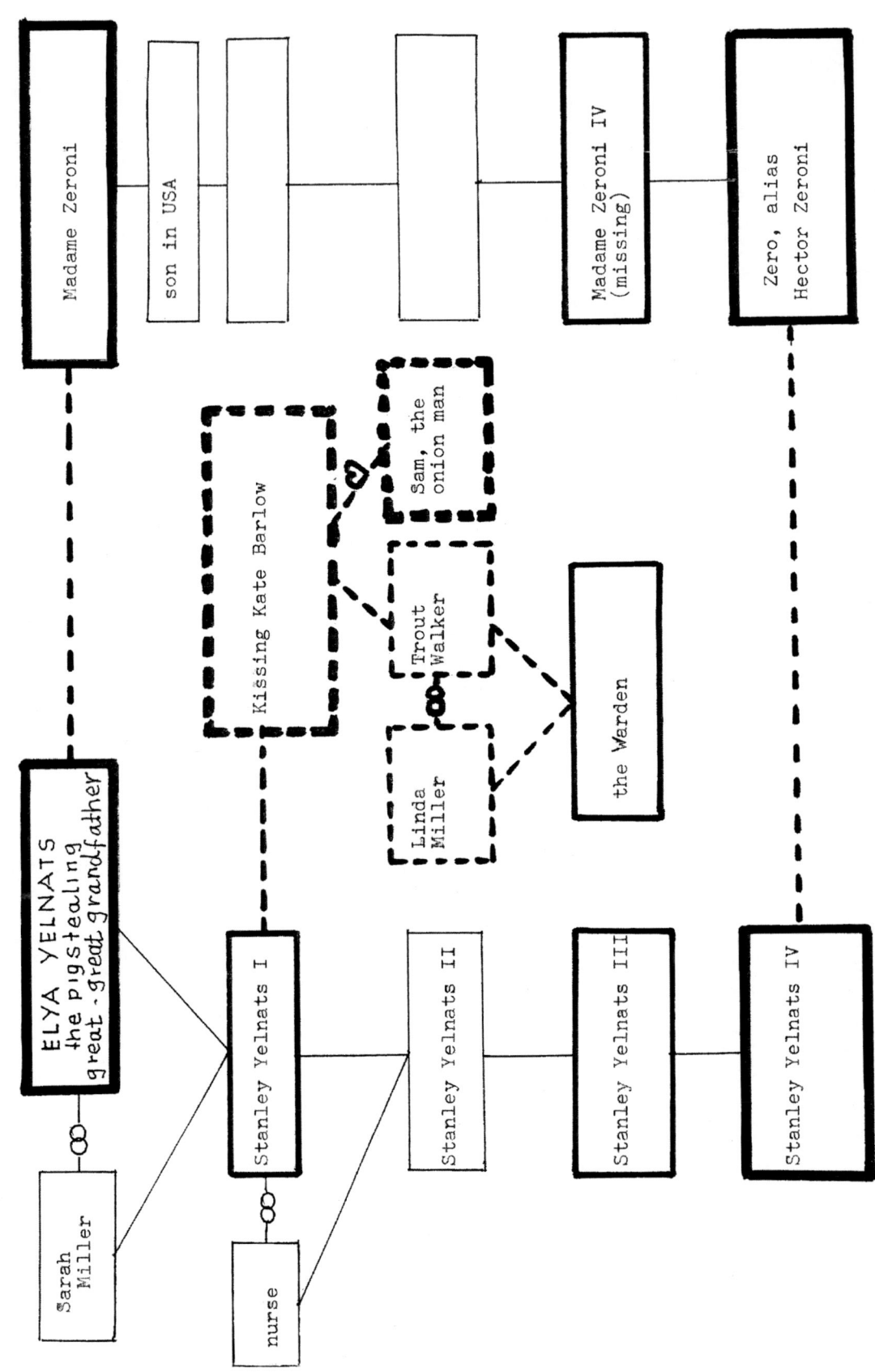

W 6 Character files

W 6.1 X-Ray

Tent D Name/nickname: Rex/X-Ray Photo	Date of arrival	almost a year ago (41)
	Date of release	
	Crime/misdemeanor	
	Age	
	Skin color	black (17)
	Outward appearance	wears glasses (17) second smallest of the boys (42)
	Behavior in the camp	first in line for water (40), leader of the group (41) He pretends to have found a gold tube (49) and gets the rest of the day off, a double shower and some clean clothes.
	Other	plays pool (35) origin of nickname: pig Latin (41)

W 6.2 Squid

Tent D Name/nickname: Alan/Squid Photo	Date of arrival	
	Date of release	
	Crime/misdemeanor	
	Age	
	Skin color	white (17)
	Outward appearance	
	Behavior in the camp	third in line for water (40) works with Magnet (51) does not want to admit that he cries at night (59)
	Other	

W 6.3 Armpit

Tent D Name/nickname: Theodore/Armpit Photo	Date of arrival	
	Date of release	
	Crime/misdemeanor	
	Age	
	Skin color	black (59)
	Outward appearance	next to Stanley biggest of the boys (42)
	Behavior in the camp	second in line for water (40) trustworthy (19) plays pool (35) best friend with Rex Zigzag and Armpit dig together (51) Armpit provokes the Warden so that she has to jab at him with her pitchfork, knocking him backward into the big hole. The fork leaves three holes in the front of this shirt and three tiny spots of blood (56). Comes to rescue Zigzag from Zero's choking grips (91).
	Other	

W 6.4 Magnet

Tent D Name/nickname: José/Magnet Photo	Date of arrival	
	Date of release	
	Crime/misdemeanor	
	Age	
	Skin color	Hispanic (59)
	Outward appearance	
	Behavior in the camp	fifth in line for water (40) works with Squid (51) Stole sunflower seeds (60) but this is not sure because they were found in Stanley's hole.
	Other	likes animals (43) would like to be an animal trainer (43) origin of nickname: his fingers are like magnets, i.e. he tends to steal things (60)

W 6.5 Zigzag

Tent D Name/nickname: Ricky/Zigzag/Ziggy Photo	Date of arrival	has been in the camp for 46 days (88)
	Date of release	
	Crime/misdemeanor	
	Age	his birthday is on July 8th (87)
	Skin color	white (59)
	Outward appearance	long skinny neck, big round head with wild frizzy blond hair that sticks out in all directions (32) Slightly taller than Armpit because of his long neck (42)
	Behavior in the camp	fourth in line for water (40) Zigzag and Armpit work/dig together (51) his shovel catches Stanley in the side of his head (56) provokes Stanley (90), hits Stanley hard on the shoulder with his open hand, challenges Stanley and hits him and finally pushes him into a hole and jumps on top of him (91) Zero stops him. (91)
	Other	

W 6.6 Caveman

Tent D Name/nickname: Stanley/Caveman Photo	Date of arrival	May 24th (87)
	Date of release	released by court order the day he returns to the camp (140)
	Crime/misdemeanor	stole a pair of sneakers which belonged to Clyde Livingston, a famous baseball player
	Age	
	Skin color	white (59)
	Outward appearance	overweight (24) lost some weight and has well adjusted to harsh conditions (88)
	Behavior in the camp	Seventh in line for water (40), then sixth in line for water (48) finds a fossil (40) quickly gets a nickname, accepted by the group (42) digs with Zero (51)

		hurt by Zigzag's shovel on the side of his head: blood and a big gash below his ear (56f.); bandaged with a piece of burlap; goes back to work after the incident (57) works nearly as fast as Magnet (57) admits that he has stolen a bag of sunflower seeds and is taken to the Warden (62); might he covering up for X-Ray or someone else (62) the Warden runs her sharp wet fingernails with the poisonous rattlesnake polish down his cheek (63) starts teaching Zero to read and write (67); Zero helps him dig his hole in return; this leads to tensions with the rest of the group (89) and to a fight with Zigzag (90) claims not to know where Zero has disappeared to (96) steals camp truck and drives but straight into a hole (98f.), then runs off with an empty canteen is found early one morning more than a week after his escape digging up treasure in a hole; digs up nest of dangerous lizards (133f.) is released by court order (140) allowed to keep the suitcase he dug up because his name is written on it (141)
	Other	writes letters home (37, 58) and receives letters (54) from his parents

W 6.7 Zero

Tent D	Date of arrival	no more than a month or two before Stanley (122)
Name/nickname: Hector Zeroni/Zero	**Date of release**	released together with Stanley
	Crime/misdemeanor	stole a pair of shoes from a store (121)
	Age	
	Skin color	black (59)
Photo	**Outward appearance**	second smallest (31) usually has an angry expression on his face (44, 45) occasionally has a "huge smile" (44)
	Behavior in the camp	so stupid he does not even know he is stupid (93) sixth in line for water (40), later seventh in line for water (48) no plans for the future; likes digging holes and is always the first to finish (31) finishes Stanley's hole while Stanley is with the Warden (66) digs with Stanley (51) and later digs holes for Stanley in exchange for lessons defends Stanley when Zigzag attacks him (91) attacks Mr. Pendanski with a shovel and flees into the desert without taking any water along (93) returns to the camp with Stanley after more than a week's absence (133)
	Other	is a ward of the state (96) origin of nickname: abbreviation of family name Zeroni and to indicate that he has no (zero) brains (82, 18)

W 6.8 Twitch

Tent D	Date of arrival	three days after Zero left (97)
Name/nickname: Brian/Twitch	Date of release	
	Crime/misdemeanor	stole a car (97)
	Age	
	Skin color	
Photo	Outward appearance	
	Behavior in the camp	fidgety (97), nervous takes over Zero's place and bed advises Stanley when he steals the pickup truck (98)
	Other	very good: quick and effective at stealing cars origin of nickname: so nervous he makes uncontrolled movements (97)

W 7 Character relationships

Part I: chapter 4–11

The relationships among the boys of group D are clearly defined and can be fitted into a top-down ranking. There is a leader, his two supporters, the rest, a loser, and a newcomer. The ranking which can also be seen as a line looks like this:

X-Ray
    Armpit/Squid
        Zigzag/Magnet
           Zero
             Stanley

The most powerful boy, nicknamed X-Ray, is the leader of the group (41) although he is the second smallest (42). Not only does he bear the name Rex (Latin for king, 42), he also controls the rest of the group (41), especially his "friends", Squid and Armpit. These two strictly adhere to the rules set by X-Ray concerning the ranking within the group. These three have certain rituals – like spitting into the hole when the digging is finished (32) – and make sure the others follow these rules, too.

Next in the ranking come Zigzag, Magnet, and Zero. Zigzag does not play an important role at all, whereas Magnet is definitely not taken seriously by Squid when he mocks at him by telling the group that he thinks Magnet belongs in a zoo (43). This utterance shows how hurtful and powerful Squid can be in order to re-establish his position among the group members. He can be sure of X-Ray's and Armpit's support. He also makes fun of Stanley because he writes letters to his mother (37).

Neither do we learn much about Zero. He is the smallest in the group and comes last (42). He stares at the letter when Stanley writes home (38) but does not try to establish any verbal communication with him beyond asking him a detail about the shoes that dropped on Stanley and led to his arrest. Stanley, the newcomer, quickly senses that his arrival in the camp has attracted the strongest and the weakest group member. While X-Ray readily displays his power, Zero seems in a way fascinated by Stanley (37f.).

After the first day, Stanley realizes that he had better not make X-Ray angry by telling him about the injustice with which he rules the inmates (36f.). He does not want to run the risk of losing X-Ray's acceptance: he is glad to have been welcomed as a group member when they give him a nickname (41) and when he is called "cool" (Armpit: 36) or "one tough dude" (Squid: 36). Compared with the humiliation he has known in school at the hands of Derrick, he thinks X-Ray's rule is still bearable.

This is why he hands over his second find, the gold tube, to X-Ray. His reluctance to accept X-Ray as the leader of the group, however, can be seen in the fact that he does not point out to X-Ray that the tube has an engraving (47). It is when he tells X-Ray that he would have more of a day off if he pretended to have found the gold tube the following morning that he moves up in the lunch line and changes places with Zero.

So one can say that the lunchline is set up according to the number and importance of favours done X-Ray. The new ranking looks like this:

X-Ray
    Armpit-Squid
        Zigzag- Magnet
           Stanley
             Zero.

Part II: Chapters 14–22

In the second half of Part Two this newly established ranking does not change. What emerges though is the underlying struggle for power and dominance and, at the same time, the desperation and loneliness which all become manifest either in the boys' harsh verbal exchanges or even physical attacks.

X-Ray reaffirms his position of power when he celebrates his success (53) because he "tricked" Mr. Sir with the gold tube and thus makes the others feel inferior to him (cf. Zigzag's comments on X-Ray's gloating). He still controls the communication processes. For this he – as the leader – does not allow any contradiction (53) and he again makes sure that neither his respect nor that of a favored group member is threatened. This becomes clear, for example, when he tells Mr. Sir that Stanley's name is Caveman (54). He also defends Stanley against his "friends" Squid and Armpit when they start mocking at him because he received a letter from his mother (54). He also has the right to snap at the other boys without any obvious reason (48).

Armpit and Squid are still X-Ray's most loyal companions. But both envy Stanley because he has got a mother who cares and therefore writes back to him (54). It is Squid who is homesick in the night after Stanley gets a letter from home (59). But instead of admitting his feelings of loneliness and desperation, he is very aggressive toward Stanley the next morning. Although Armpit does not cry in the night, he also seems to be extremely sensitive and full of envy and curiosity when it comes to any relationships outside Camp Green Lake (54).

As long as X-Ray stands by him (53), Stanley can cope with the verbal transgressions of Armpit and Squid. Things change, however, when it comes to physical attacks by Zigzag. First he hits Stanley with his shovel (56) saying he would not dig his dirt up. Only Magnet helps Stanley to his feet (57). Then Zigzag throws the sack of sunflower seeds at him, but since he hadn't closed the sack, the seeds are spilled all over the place in Stanley's hole (60). When Stanley returns from the Warden, his hole has almost been finished. He still thinks the group is on his side (66) when he thanks them. It is only then that he comes to realize that he has "lost" them but for two members: Magnet who again expresses his respect ("good going": 66) and Zero who is the one who almost finished digging Stanley's hole (66).

This incident is a decisive step for both of them: Zero wins Stanley's attention and respect. He then dares to tell him that he hates playing this game of power and humiliation according to X-Ray's or anybody else's rules. That is the reason why he would not answer their stupid questions. It is only when Stanley is deceived by X-Ray and frees himself from his game of power and favors that he comes to acknowledge and appreciate Zero. From the two members of the boy's group in Tent D who both wanted Stanley's admiration and attention it is eventually Zero who wins!

W 8 Steps to friendship
See page 18.

W 9 Stanley writes a letter to his mother

June 21, 2002

Dear Mom,

Today was my first day at camp, and I've already made some friends. We've been out on the lake all day, so I'm pretty tired. Once I pass the swimming test I'll get to learn how to water-ski.

Tomorrow some of my new friends and I will do some gardening in the park which surrounds the camp buildings. After a day's work, we will be really tired but also very satisfied with ourselves, I'm sure.

Luckily, the food here is fantastic: Cereals, pancakes or eggs and fresh orange juice for breakfast, and a plentiful meal in the evening.

How's Dad's sneaker project coming along? I miss you but I don't miss the odor in the apartment! It always reminds me of that nursery rhyme about the old woman who lived in a shoe. Do you remember it?

There was an old woman who lived in a shoe,
She had so many children she didn't know what to do;
She gave them some broth without any bread,
And whipped them all soundly and put them to bed.

Well, I'll go to bed now, too. Say hello to Dad. I hope you are doing fine.

Hope to be back soon.
Love,
Stanley

Stanley & Zero - Steps to Friendship

Stanley

<= two outsiders =>

Zero

no friends at home
overweight
bullied at school

stands in line behind
Zero

mentions pig-
stealing great-great
grandfather (44)

stands in line in front of Zero

Stanley asks Zero about
nursery rhymes

refuses to teach
Zero to read

never thanks Zero
for digging his hole
(66)

thanks Zero (67)

offers Zero to teach him to
read

agrees to Zero's deal

bullied and beaten up by
ZigZag (90)

angry at himself but doesn't go out
after Zero

very worried about Zero (142)

all his thoughts form on Zero: What if he is still
alive? (98)

decides to find Zero, steals truck

finds Zero under the boat

they try to reach Big Thumb

carries Zero up the mountain

there is nothing inside his
head (18)
smallest kid
"a weird dude"

the first to finish digging
(31)

realizes that he has stolen the
sneakers Stanley was arrested
for (46)

even Zero smiles

has never watched Sesame Street

asks Stanley to teach him to read and
write (58)

digs Stanley's hole while he is at the Warden's

tells Stanley that Stanley didn't steal the sneakers
(67)

accepts Stanley's offer happily

offers a deal: He will dig part of Stanley's hole in return

is a quick learner (80)

tells Stanley that his real name is Hector Zeroni

helps Stanley and saves him

runs away after being humiliated by Mom

does not return

more information on Zero (96)

shares his last Sploosh with Stanley

they try to reach Big Thumb

manages to pull up Stanley on a ledge bearing the
pain of bleeding gashes in his hands

confesses that he stole the sneakers

they share their last water on their way back to the camp

they tell each other about their past

they find the treasure (132)

they become rich and happy

W 10 Kate Barlow's Story

Step 1: Corrected statements

d) Trout Walker was one of Ms. Barlow's **night-school** students.

g) Kate came back to Green Lake and lived in an abandoned **cabin**, where she mourned Sam.

h) One day Kate Barlow asked Sam to help her repair the roof of the **schoolhouse**.

i) Sam and Kate tried to escape in Sam's boat but were chased by Trout Walker's **motor boat**.

o) He cured people of illnesses with his **onion juice**.

p) 20 years later Green Lake was just a little pond of **dirty** water.

s) Sam was not allowed to attend classes because he was a **Negro**.

Step 2: Sequence of events

1	2	3	4	5	6	7	8	9	10	11	12	13	14	15	16	17	18	19	20	21	22	23	24	25	26
b	n	q	u	d	f	w	e	o	h	s	l	r	k	m	a	j	z	i	c	t	x	p	g	v	y

b) 110 years ago Green Lake was the largest lake in Texas.

n) Kate Barlow, a pretty young woman, lived at the edge of the lake.

q) She was the town's only teacher.

u) Kate also taught classes in the evenings for adults.

d) Trout Walker was one of Ms Barlow's night-school students.

f) One day Trout invited Kate to a ride in his motor boat, which she refused.

w) He was a lot more interested in the teacher than in getting an education.

e) Sam, the onion seller, who often passed by the schoolhouse, went around with a cart drawn by his donkey Mary Lou.

o) He cured people from illnesses with his onion juice.

h) One day Kate Barlow asked Sam to help her repair the roof of the schoolhouse.

s) Sam was not allowed to attend classes because he was a Negro.

l) Kate enjoyed watching Sam do some odd jobs around the schoolhouse.

r) By the end of the term Sam had turned the old run-down schoolhouse into a little jewel which the whole town was proud of.

k) When Sam said goodbye, Kate hugged Mary Lou's neck saying that her heart was breaking.

m) Then Sam took hold of Kate's hand and kissed her.

a) Although there was no telephone in the village, the news of Sam kissing Kate spread like wildfire.

j) The following morning no kid came to school at all.

z) The sheriff wanted to hang Onion Sam for kissing a white woman.

i) Sam and Kate tried to escape in Sam's boat but were chased by Trout Walker's motor boat.

c) Sam was shot and killed in the water and Kate was rescued against her wishes.

t) Three days after Sam's death, Kate shot the sheriff and became an outlaw who robbed all kinds of rich people for the next 20 years.

x) Since then not one drop of rain has fallen on Green Lake.

p) 20 years later Green Lake was just a little pond of dirty water.

g) Kate came back to Green Lake and lived in an abandoned cabin, where she mourned Sam.

v) Trout Walker and his wife were desperate to get Kate's loot, which she had gathered while being an outlaw, and mistreated her severely.

y) Finally a lizard killed Kate, who told Trout and Linda to start digging for the treasure she had hidden in the ground and then died laughing.

Step 3: Historical narration
(all connectives printed in bold type)

110 years ago Green Lake, on whose edge Kate Barlow, a pretty young woman and the town's only teacher, lived, was the largest lake in Texas. Kate also taught classes in the evenings for adults, **one of whom** was Trout Walker. One day Trout, **who** was a lot more interested in the teacher than in getting an education, invited Kate on a ride in his motor boat, **which** she refused. Sam, the onion seller, **who** cured people of illnesses with his onion juice, often passed by the schoolhouse with a cart drawn by his donkey Mary Lou.

One day Kate Barlow asked Sam to help her repair the roof of the schoolhouse. Sam, **however**, was not allowed to attend classes **because** he was a Negro. Kate enjoyed watching Sam do some odd jobs around the schoolhouse and by the end of the term Sam had turned the old run-down schoolhouse into a little jewel, **which** the whole town was proud of. When Sam said goodbye, Kate hugged Mary Lou's neck saying that her heart was breaking. Then Sam took hold of Kate's hand and kissed her.

Although there was no telephone in the village, the news of Sam kissing Kate spread like wildfire. **The following morning** no kid came to school at all. The sheriff wanted to hang Sam for kissing a white woman. **Therefore** Sam and Kate tried to escape in Sam's boat **but** were chased by Trout Walker's motor boat. **In the end** Sam was shot and killed in the water. Kate was rescued against her wishes. **As a consequence**, three days after Sam's death, Kate shot the sheriff and became an outlaw who robbed all kinds of rich people for the next 20 years.

Since then not one drop of rain has fallen on Green Lake so that 20 years later Green Lake was just a little pond of dirty water. **When** Kate came back to Green Lake, she lived in an abandoned cabin, **where** she mourned Sam. **When** Trout Walker and his wife heard about this, they were desperate to get Kate's loot, **which** she had gathered **while being** an outlaw, **and they** mistreated her severely. **Finally** a lizard killed Kate, **who** told Trout and Linda to start digging for the treasure she had hidden in the ground **and** then died laughing.

W 11 Kate Barlow Wanted poster

Wanted

for murder and robbery

dead or alive

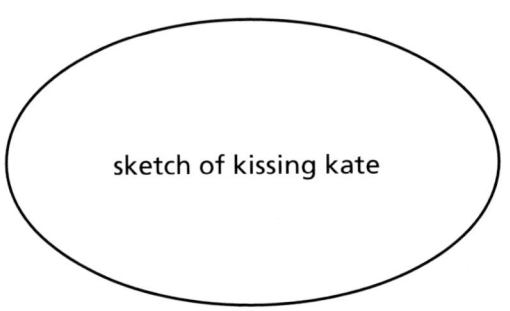

sketch of kissing kate

Kissin' Kate Barlow

- very pretty, intelligent woman
- former teacher of the town of Green Lake
- associates with Negroes
- turned crazy after her Negro boyfriend had been killed
- always applies a fresh coat of red lipstick before kissing her victims

REWARD: $10,000

The Sheriff of Green Lake, Texas

W 12 Formal letter to the Attorney General
Step 1: Note-taking: Description of the staff

	Mr. Sir	Mr. Pendanski	the Warden
outward appearance	always wears sunglasses and a cowboy hat rattlesnake tattoo on his arm	younger and not as scary looking as Mr. Sir close-shaven head, thick curly black beard, nose badly sunburned	tall red-haired woman wears a black cowboy hat and black cowboy boots with turquoise stones face and arms covered with freckles
nickname	wants to be addressed "Mr. Sir"	is called "Mom" by the boys	
favourite sentence	always mentions that Camp Green Lake is no Girl Scout camp	instructs Stanley about the one rule at the camp: "Don't upset the Warden."	only one rule at the camp: "Don't upset the Warden." "Excuse me" used in a way to underline her absolute authority
job / position	gave Stanley instructions about the camp has a position above Mr. Pendanski, but inferior to the Warden spills Stanley's water on purpose is not accountable to anybody and enjoys this privilege	counselor of tent D inferior to Mr. Sir and the Warden	very dominant: not only the boys but also Mr. Sir and Mr. Pendanski are in awe of her
habits	quit smoking and eats sunflowerseeds instead carries a gun	does not call the boys by their nicknames, prefers to call them by the names "society will recognize them by"	fingernails painted with venomous dark-red nail polish only appears when something important happens (something is found in a hole; decision how to deal with Zero's disappearance, etc.) otherwise does not want to be disturbed
attitude towards the boys	wouldn't waste a bullet on the boys; bullets only for lizards very cold, does not seem to care much for anybody else frightens the boys very aggressive: choked a boy when he stared at his swollen face	makes the boys believe that he respects and understands them wants to help the boys make something of their lives prepares them for their return to society; encourages them to believe in themselves tries to create a family atmosphere among the boys playfully makes fun of Zero at the beginning insults Zero after the riot at the hole, ridicules him thinks Zero is too stupid to learn to read	very violent and calculating (strikes Mr. Sir for disturbing her with his stolen sunflower seeds, knowing he will take revenge on Stanley) does not care for anything that does not directly concern herself

Step 2: letter

Dear Mr. Attorney General,

My name is Stanley Yelnats and I am an inmate of Camp Green Lake, a "juvenile correctional facility", as the sign outside the main office says. I do not want to complain about our daily duty of digging holes or that I am here in the first place. I am writing to you, however, to tell you that I am worried about my friend Zero, who ran away from this place. I know that it is his own fault if something happens to him out there, but that is not the reason for my writing. I am even more worried about what the guards will do to him if he returns. Therefore I will describe the counselors and the Warden so you can get an impression of them yourself. First of all, there is Mr. Sir. He is a kind of guard here at Camp Green Lake and quite an intimidating person. He keeps mentioning that we are not at a Girl Scout camp, and he makes sure we understand what he means. We are all afraid of him because he is very aggressive. I don't know if this is because he recently quit smoking or if it is just his nature. Once he even started choking one of the inmates just because the boy stared at him for too long. Although he claims that he would never use his gun on us, as shooting a boy would be a waste of bullets, we all try not to upset him and keep a low profile. The Warden is the only person Mr.Sir has to account to and since the Warden does not care about anything that does not directly involve herself, Mr. Sir can practically do whatever he likes. The Warden lives in a cabin at the camp site, which she only leaves in case something important happens. Otherwise she does not want to be disturbed. The first time I ever saw her was when something was found in one of the holes. The second time I met her I found out why, according to Mr. Pendanski, the camp's only rule is "Don't upset the Warden": Mr. Sir took me to her cabin because he thought I had stolen the sunflower seeds he eats as a substitute for smoking. Instead of punishing me, she painted her fingernails with venomous nail polish and struck Mr. Sir for disturbing her. She must have known that Mr. Sir would take revenge on me, so she is not only violent but also very calculating.
Mr. Pendanski, whom we call Mom, is the counselor of the tent I live in. He is younger than the others and not as scary looking as Mr. Sir. At the beginning I thought he was the most humane of them all as he tried to create something like a family atmosphere among the boys in my tent. He even made us believe that he understands and respects us. Maybe I should have become suspicious in one of our regular evening circles, in which we talked about our lives after Camp Green Lake. There he encouraged us to believe in ourselves, apart from Zero, of whom he made fun because of his inability to read and write. But I did not see through him until the riot at one of the holes. Mr. Pendanski insulted and ridiculed Zero badly and finally caused him to run away. Then, he did not seem to care for us, or for Zero in this case, anymore.
I am confident you understand our situation here at the camp and that there is nobody we can trust. I hope you can do something for my friend.

Yours sincerely,
Stanley Yelnats

P.S.: I overheard a conversation in which they decided to erase Zero's files from the state computers so that nobody will ask any questions. So, please, act immediately.

W 13 Advertising the camp

Camp Green Lake

The alternative institution for the improvement of "bad boys"

Most recent research has shown that young people tend to adopt appropriate social behavior more easily when they are in groups of their age under skillful guidance.

Character training in surroundings that offer challenge and adventure.
We teach young offenders to become useful, hard-working members of society.
We help them to turn their lives around. But we expect them to help, too.
Our principle is: Discipline will improve character.

Accommodation / Equipment
Our boys live in groups of seven in tents close to the lake.
Clothes and food are provided (fresh laundry every 3 days!).
Free gear is provided for our numerous excursions.

Daily schedule

Mornings	Adventure time: Sports activities, archeological and wildlife excursions (we believe in digging to build character)
Afternoons:	Back in the camp, time to relax and organized free time. TV and lots of other leisure facilities in our fully furnished RECREATION ROOM are available.
Evenings	Regular counseling sessions with our qualified staff.

CAMP GREEN LAKE – the # 1 chance for young offenders.
Give 'em a chance!

For more information write to us at the address below or go to our website
www.camp-green-lake.com

W 14 Interior monologue: Stanley's new sense of self

Wow, what's that? It's flowing through my body. Believe it or not, I think I'm happy. I can't remember having had this feeling before. Most of my life I was unhappy. I can see myself, big, fat, and lonely. I didn't dare to talk to the others because I thought I'm not worth talking to. Some teachers made fun of me, I think they didn't even realize it. It hurt a lot, though. Oh and Derrick Dunne, this little rat, I complained to the teachers, look, he's bullying me, but they just laughed. I was much bigger, so why didn't I fight back – I don't know. Now I would: I feel much stronger and my friends would help me; remember how they defended me when that big fellow provoked me (36), that was a great feeling. Yes, I'm in good shape now. At first I thought I'd never make it, but I kept on, step by step and now I've even been on top of Big Thumb; I've become tough. Zero is my best friend. I still feel ashamed when I think about the way I first treated him. I thought I was nothing, and that Zero was nothing, but he is worse off than me. When Zigzag and the others attacked me, I still wasn't able to fight back. Zero saved me, and then he ran away. I had to help him, I had to find him! How did I have the courage to steal Mr. Sir's car? I'd never done anything like that before. I know I'm able to do a lot of things, Zero has helped me to find that out. I think I like myself now.

W 15 Interview with Stanley's father

The Story of SPLOOSH

Thousands of people in this country suffer from foot odor. And it's not only they who suffer – it's their families, friends, sports mates, simply everybody who comes into contact with the person removing his or her shoes. Stanley Yelnats III invented the cure: *Sploosh*. **Science Today** interviewed the inventor.

Science Today: Mr Yelnats, what inspired you to invent a product which eliminates foot odor? Do you suffer from athlete's foot yourself?

Stanley Yelnats III: No, I don't. I actually wanted to find a way to recycle old sneakers. I was sure that if somebody found a use for old sneakers, this person would become rich.

Science Today: So you discovered the formula for *Sploosh* by accident?

Stanley Yelnats III: I don't believe that there is anything like "accident" or "coincidence". To be a successful inventor you need three things: Intelligence, perseverance and a little bit of luck. I have always had the first two, but I just lacked the little bit of luck. Yet I remained hopeful that one day the curse would be removed from our family.

Science Today: The curse?

Stanley Yelnats III: Oh yes, my family has been cursed for four generations. My great-grandfather Elya once received a pig from a gypsy woman in Latvia. In return she wanted him to carry her up a mountain and sing a special song to her. She cursed him and all his descendants because my great-grandfather broke his promise. Since then, my family has always had bad luck.

Science Today: And now that you invented *Sploosh* the curse is removed?

Stanley Yelnats III: No, it's the other way round: Because the curse had been removed, I was able to invent *Sploosh*.

Science Today: I see. You said you don't believe in accidents. What else led to your invention?

Stanley Yelnats III: It was destiny! Some people might say that the story I am going to tell you now is based on coincidence. But there were far too many coincidences not to believe in destiny. You see, my son Stanley had always been bullied at school. One day his notebook was thrown into the toilet and it took him such a long time to retrieve it that he missed the bus and had to walk home. When he was just walking out from under a freeway overpass, a pair of sneakers fell from the sky. Knowing about my project, Stanley wanted to take the sneakers home, but unfortunately it turned out that they were the sneakers Clyde "Sweet Feet" Livingston had donated to help raise money for a homeless shelter. So Stanley was arrested and taken to a juvenile correctional facility in the Texan desert. There he did not only meet the person who really stole the sneakers, he also carried him up a mountain to save his new friend's life, as well as his own. He even sang him the song that had been sung as a lullaby to all the children in our family. I don't want to bore you by telling you all the details of the story, although there were even more coincidences. The most important point is that Stanley's new friend is the great-great-great-grandson of Madame Zeroni, the gypsy woman who put a curse on our family.

Science Today: I see. And this removed the family curse...

Stanley Yelnats III: ...and enabled me to invent *Sploosh*.

Science Today: Does the product's name, *Sploosh*, have a particular meaning?

Stanley Yelnats III: It does not exactly have a meaning, but destiny is involved here again. You know, Stanley and his friend ran away from the camp and went to that mountain in the middle of the desert without food or water. They only survived because they found some spiced preserved peaches, which they called *Sploosh*, under a boat. And since my spray against foot odor smells like peaches they thought it might be a nice idea to call it *Sploosh*, too.

Science Today: Mr Yelnats, tell us how *Sploosh* works.

Stanley Yelnats III: Well, actually it is quite simple . . .

W 16 TV script for a Sploosh commercial

For this exercise students, who are usually TV experts, might be more creative than teachers. Therefore, this should be a totally free assignment without any rules or patterns to follow.

W 17 Zero's report on the development of his friendship

Zero and his mother eventually find time to talk about his experiences at Camp Green Lake. Zero tells her how he came to know his best friend Stanley better. In his report he explains to her the difficult beginning and the ups and downs of their friendship.

Take the diagram (W 8) as a basis and highlight those steps in the ups and downs of the friendship which you consider to be important before you actually start to write.

I had been at Camp Green Lake for a while. Nobody really liked me. I was always last in the lunch line. But I thought **it'd be no use fighting** against the leader, X-Ray. I was the smallest anyway and I would not have known how to fight them with words because X-Ray and his gang had their own logic. They laughed at me and said things like "There's nothing inside his head" (18). Long before they said it, I had felt it and because I didn't want any trouble I had decided not **to react to** their provocations. **This is when** they started calling me "weird". But I was always first to finish digging my hole (p. 31) – you know, we had to dig these stupid holes, a hole a day!

Then one day a new boy came to the camp. It was Stanley. Of course, everybody was **interested in** who he was and why he was there. And, of course, he had to take the last position in the lunch line. For once, I was only second last.

He said strange things about his great-great-grandfather; actually he called him "My no-good-dirty-rotten-pig-stealing-great-great-grandfather"(44). That was really funny because nobody had expected him to say anything like this. I will never forget this.

He also mentioned something about sneakers falling from the sky. Everybody thought he was a bit **strange, but still** X-Ray began to like him, too. And suddenly **I was last in line** again. When I tried to talk to Stanley, his answers were very short **as if he wanted** to get rid of me. But I needed to find out about the sneakers. And, would you believe it, it was the very same pair of sneakers I had stolen and then put on top of a parked car. They must have fallen off the car and landed on Stanley's head! What a **coincidence!**

I saw that Stanley received letters from his parents and that he wrote them back. I was really envious and I thought if only I could write and read and ... maybe he would teach me. When I **suggested** this to him he did not like it. He laughed me full in the face and found an easy excuse saying something like he did not know how to teach. I insisted but he was really cold. I was very sad because I had thought that he would be the only person in the group I'd really like to talk to. I did not know what to do.

Everything changed when Stanley got into trouble and was taken to the Warden. It was a **trap** set by the other boys in the group. I never quite understood what was going on in their minds but they were somewhat full of mischief. While Stanley was at the Warden's, I dug his hole. He was really touched to see it almost finished when he returned. I then thought that maybe I'd have another chance to tell him that he didn't steal the sneakers because I stole them. I only managed to tell him that he had not stolen the sneakers. Stanley seemed quite grateful to me for having dug his hole, and we **made a deal**: Every day I would dig part of his hole, he could take a rest in the meantime and save some energy for the evening when he would teach me to read and write.

After the first lesson I was very **pleased with** myself. I was a better learner than I was way back in school. **What a relief** to realize that I would finally learn to read and write! I would be able to understand so much more of the world!

Unfortunately, the others soon found out about our deal and started to **tease** him. Then, one morning, Stanley was beaten up by Zigzag and I don't know what would have happened if I had not saved him.

Then the going got tough: One of the two men, a counselor we called Mom, said really nasty things to me and **I couldn't stand** it anymore. It was just too much. I just ran away with that empty canteen. I did not care. I could not take any more of it. I was fed up. I had had enough of the others and now this counselor humiliating me. I did not want to return to the camp ever.

I stayed out there in the desert for three days and I told you before what it looks like. There is nothing. The sun always shines and it gets so hot and I did not have any water and I thought I would die, but it was still better than returning to the camp. I found a boat and under the boat I found sixteen jars of what must have been preserved peaches. I called the preserve Sploosh and I lived on this for three days.

Then Stanley turned up! I was so happy to see him. He had a very worried and tired look. And he had forgotten his canteen, too. We were so thirsty. Then I decided to open the last of the jars and we shared the last of the Sploosh.

Stanley wanted me to return to the camp but I refused. I told him that Barf Bag had committed suicide by stepping on a rattlesnake. He had taken off his shoe and sock first to make sure he would die. I told Stanley that I'd rather die than return to the camp.

We moved on, we just kept walking for hours. Stanley could hardly walk anymore and there was a point when I thought I was dying and then he carried me up the mountain. On top of the mountain Stanley found water and onions that we fed on. He sang a song to me that I knew. That was really strange because I remembered having heard it before. Then I confessed to him what I had long wanted to tell him: that I had stolen Clyde Livingston's sneakers. I fed on onions and my health gradually improved.

After about a week on top of the mountain we walked back to the camp. We got close to the camp at night. I stole some water and food from the camp and Stanley started digging. We were determined to find the treasure. And we found it! There were some lizards down in the hole with us but we just kept immobile. I knew that if we were patient enough they would leave.

W 18 The Pig Lullaby – If only, if only

The questions below are meant for classroom discussion and prepare for the creative writing exercise.

Comprehension questions

1. Why does the woodpecker sigh and why does the wolf cry to the moon?
   Describe the two animals' feelings in the song and the situation they are in.
   Both woodpecker and wolf are rather unhappy with their

situation, as they haven't eaten anything for quite a while and seem to have trouble with finding food.

The woodpecker sighs because he is longing for softer bark which would enable him to get to some edible larvae or insects more easily, whereas the wolf, feeling hungry and lonely himself and finally weary with all that waiting below, begs the moon to help him get to his "woodpecker meal".

2. Is there any help from the moon or anyone else around?
The focus is on the two animals somewhere beneath the sky so that one gets the impression as if they were alone, the only creatures in the world, esp. as the moon, the only one to be addressed, does not reply but only reminds them of their loneliness / transitoriness and happier times long gone by.

Analysis

3. Who do you feel more pity or sympathy for, the woodpecker or the wolf? Give reasons.
Though the wolf is the predator and the woodpecker its prey one doesn't particularly sympathize with the weaker animal that is to be eaten, as both animals seem to be in the same desperate situation.

4. Outline when and by whom the different stanzas of the song are sung or in which context they come to Stanley's mind. Describe the respective situations.
(1ˢᵗ stanza, p.11) In the bus on his way to the camp Stanley is thinking of the curse that has always been on him and his parents, who – like him – were always "in the wrong place at the wrong time". In view of the vast emptiness ahead he remembers the song *his father used to sing to him* with its sweet and sad melody.

(2ⁿᵈ stanza, p.33) The origins of the family curse and the Latvian pig lullaby are described. (pp.25–27)
Madame Zeroni teaches Stanley's great-great-grandfather Elya that special song to sing to the piglet she has given to him. This piglet is to drink from the mysterious stream on top of a mountain and so become fat in order to win him the love of his beloved Myra. In return Elya has to promise to carry Madame Zeroni up the same mountain and to sing the same song to her, otherwise he and his descendants will be doomed forever. But the plan doesn't work out and a disappointed Elya sails off to America forgetting all about his promise to Madame Zeroni. (p.31) There he falls in love with a woman named *Sarah Miller*, who likes the pig lullaby so much that she rearranges Elya's translation, makes the English version rhyme and *sings it to their little son Stanley* (Stanley's great-grandfather) every night.

(1ˢᵗ/3ʳᵈ stanza, p.116) Hungry, thirsty, sick and totally exhausted Stanley and Zero reach the foot of Big Thumb. Here, within arm's reach of their aim and in the face of death, Zero confesses to Stanley that it was he who stole Clyde Livingston's shoes, a theft Stanley was accused of and punished for. Now *Stanley softly sings* the old family lullaby *to Zero* hoping to relieve his friend's pain.

(4ᵗʰ stanza, p.152) Because Stanley, the great-great-grandson of Elya Yelnats, carried Zero, the great-great-grandson of Madame Zeroni, up the mountain and actually saved his life, the old promise is fulfilled and the family curse is lifted at last. Stanley's and Zero's lives have turned out for the best in every respect. At a party at Clyde Livingston's to celebrate their success and reconciliation *a woman (Zero's mother or his grandmother) tenderly sings the lullaby to Zero*.

5. What do these different situations have in common?
The song is always sung in a very tender and soft way to soothe and console people, esp. children, or to show them some kind of love, protection and support. Accordingly Stanley sings it to Zero at the foot of Big Thumb when Zero is hardly alive anymore and both of them desperately need encouragement and hope. On approaching the camp the song comes to Stanley's mind as he feels frightened and completely forlorn. Being on his own with no one around to comfort him, just remembering the melody and his father's gruff voice is sufficient to give him the necessary consolation. The other two occasions both reflect the deep and genuine love a mother feels towards her child …

6. Who do you think could be the speaker in the last stanza?
A mother singing to her sad, tired, discouraged child, expressing her love and comforting it.

Formal analysis

7. Stylistic means (repetition, anaphora, direct address, …)
Rhyme pattern (ab cc or aa bb or aa bc)

Step 1: Wishes and desires

Stanley	to have a friend
	to be freed from the curse
	not to be bullied
	to be strong
Stanley's father	to be freed from the curse
	to be a successful inventor
Kate Barlow	to get rid of Trout Walker / the sheriff
	to be allowed to love Sam
	to take revenge
the Warden	to become rich
	to find the treasure
Madame Zeroni	eternal life
Zero	to be able to read and write
	to be accepted in a group
	to find his mother

Step 2: Rewriting the song/poem
"If only, if only," **Stanley Yelnats** sighs,
"I could do away with the old Yelnats' lies!
No friends, no luck, I'm miserable and lonely.
The price is so high! If only, if only."

"If only, if only," **the father** sighs,
"Elya hadn't stolen the pig from under her eyes
My smelly shoes wouldn't make me lonely."
He cries to the moo–oo–oon, "If only, if only."

"If only, if only," **the Warden** sighs,
"The treasure were found a little more quickly,
Then I could leave the camp, rich and wealthy!"
But she cries to the moo–oo–oon, "If only, if only!"

"If only, if only," **Madame Zeroni** sighs,
"I could drink from the stream and be close to the skies!
I want to get up to the mountain and only
Elya must sing to me "If only, if only!"

"If only, if only," **Kate Barlow** sighs,
"My love for Sam would break the ice,
While I'm waiting for him, hungry and lonely
Crying out loud, If only, if only!"

"If only, if only," Stanley's friend **Zero** cries,
"Stanley could teach me to read and to write,
I wouldn't be here and wouldn't be lonely
And neither would I cry, If only, if only!"

3.2 Post-reading worksheets

To find the most recent information about real bootcamps, let students do internet research first by giving out some of the addresses from the bibliography or using search engines. An interesting German source is the film "Bootcamp: Jugendstrafvollzug auf amerikanisch".

Documentary: *Bootcamp: Jugendstrafvollzug auf amerikanisch*

The 20-minute documentary deals with one juvenile correction facility in the U.S.A. It shows the absolutely authoritarian prison-like boot camp which juvenile first-time offenders have chosen over a regular 3-year prison term. The film is an example of how shock treatment and military drill lead to final submissiveness of the 20-some-year-old inmates, who are subjected to constant humiliation. The film claims that the recidivism rate is smaller than in regular prisons, a figure that is not supported by other statistics (cf. the data of the National Mental Health Association, http://www.nmha.org/go/boot-camps).

W 19 After watching the documentary, summarize its content.

Step one: add more words to the following list

institution:	people	actions / methods	aims
prison jail juvenile corrections facility boot camp	first-time offenders inmates juvenile delinquents prisoners guards wardens	shock treatment military style training to serve a prison term to be imprisoned, to be exposed to military drillconfrontations shouting, listening, to break someone's will to bully to stand, bear (ertragen) the drill to be moved to tears, to act out one's authority aggression to abuse s.o.	to break the inmates' will to shock inmates for life to lower the recidivism rate (*Rückfallquote*) to save money by shorter sentences to turn inmates into obedient citizens behavior change rehabilitation obedience order discipline submission (Unterwerfung) submissiveness (Unter-würfigkeit) effective punishment

Step 2: Write a summary using the words from the above list and the following summary elements.

The documentary *Bootcamp – Jugendstrafvollzug auf amerikanisch* deals with a real camp in the U.S.A. today. It shows older juvenile delinquents who are exposed to a military style treatment that aims at breaking the inmates' will by humiliating them. Methods like shouting and namecalling and chasing inmates through the mud and having them climb over high obstacles are the rule. The aim is to shock the young people for life, which is said to finally make them change their behavior for life. Strictest discipline is supposed to lead to submission and submissiveness. The adherents of boot camps claim that this is a most effective method of reducing the recidivism rate.

W 20 The guards in the documentary and in the novel: a comparison

Step 1: Make an outline of the similarities and differences:	**A Similarities** 1. control over inmates 2. one inmate cannot bear the harsh rules (Zero, …) 3. **B Differences** 1. The Warden is the highest authority. 2. The guards in Holes don't shout, are more sarcastic, wish to break kids is not foremost. 3. The guards in Holes are more human (e.g. pme of them is trying to give up smoking). 4. Camp Green Lake's rules are not approved by the law.
Step 2: Topic sentence: Write the most general statement at the beginning:	When I look at the role of the guards in Holes and in the documentary *Bootcamp* I realize a few similarities, but more differences.
Step 3: Decide in which format you want to structure your essay. If you want to analyze the similarities in one go and then look at the differences, you should write at least two different paragraphs. If, however, you compare point by point, several paragraphs will be the result.	
Step 4: Start with one of the two categories: Step 5: Give at least one example of this statement:	Looking at the similarities one can see that both types of guards have (or at least at first seem to have) absolute control over the kids' lives: for example, Stanley is given no more water after Mr. Sir has been punished by the warden… Another example of the guards' total control is that they just erase Zero's file from the computer when …
An example of point-by-point comparison:	However, the two male guards in *Holes* totally depend on the female Warden, who seems to have uncontrolled power over them. She not only determines what has to be done at the camp, but also punishes the men physically. This is illustrated when she scratches Mr. Sir's face with her poisonous nail polish… (One has of course to be aware of the fact that the figure of the Warden's is part of the unrealistic, fantastic, tall-tale elements of the story, whose main goal is not to show real life at a real boot camp.)

W 21 Panel discussion: How effective are boot camps?

By way of preparation for the panel discussion students are asked to read the text "Bootcamps – are they effective?" (see additional material) before designing their role cards.

4. Further assignments and mini projects

Indidivdual tasks
Stanley's development
Zero's and Stanley's friendship
The hierarchy in the camp: the relationships among the inmates
The relationships among the counselors
Black and white in the camp and in Texas 110 years ago
The Yelnats and the Zeronis: a family history and a family tree
Kate Barlow and the West
Irony in the novel

Research Project
Juvenile boot camps in the United States
Juvenile delinquency in the United States

Illiteracy – a universal problem
Segregation
Desertification in Texas
Race relations in Texas
Segregation at the turn of the 20th century
The climate of Texas
Dangers of the desert: flora and fauna
Reptiles
Homelessness
Legendary outlaws
The Wild West
Women in the Wild West (Cat Ballou, Annie Oakley
The history of Texas

5. Assessment

Assessment by the teacher

Students have been exposed to all kinds of text types (cf. p. 7 table of text types) and should be able to produce a few in a class test. As producing those text types hass been practised, one of them or similar ones should be chosen for essay paper assignments. The teacher could either choose different situations and perspectives from the ones presented in this guide, or should just leave out one assignment and keep it for a test.

Essay paper criteria

To assess students' writing performance in essay test papers the following criteria sheet could be used:
Example: letter to the attorney
Purpose: to inform the AG about the management of the camp and to ask for supervision
Addressee: Attorney General
Style: formal English, connectives, transitions, specific vocabulary

6. The film

Distributor:	Walt Disney Pictures	
Director:	Andrew Davis	
Producers:	Phoenix Pictures	
Screenplay:	Louis Sachar	
Director of photography	Stephen St. John	
Music	Joel McNeely	
Editors	Tom Nordberg, Jeffrey Wolf	
Cast:	Shia LaBeouf	Stanley
	Sigourney Weaver,	Warden
	Jon Voight	Mr. Sir
	Tim Blake Nelson	Dr. Pendanski
	Eartha Kitt	Madame Zeroni
	Patricia Arquette	Kate
	Henry Winkler	Stanley's Father
	Siobhan Fallon	Stanleys Mother
	Dule Hill	Sam
	Khelo Thomas	Zero
Running time:	117 minutes	

The film was by and large favorably reviewed (e.g. in *The New York Times, Chicago Sun Times, www.newsday.com,* etc.). A negative review is found in *The Seattle Post-Intelligencer* April 18, 2003, reviewer William Arnold judging the movie to be "too shallow and dark for its young audiences".
The review by Wilson Morales (blackfilm.com) praises Sachar's screenplay, which enables the audience to understand the rather complicated plot and sub-plots. He praises Davis, the director for weaving the several stories into the film without making it too convoluted. He praises the acting of all the actors, especially of Shia LaBeouf in his first major role and above all, he praises the messages of love, teamwork, friendship, and trust, all making the film "very enjoyable and a pleasure to watch".
In order to make the film more accessible in the EFL classroom, a brief survey of the film is given here, which teachers may use as a reference. The sheet "film terminology" (p. 59) is to serve as a reference for both students and teachers.

6.1 Overview

sections	images, content	music, special effects, film language
opening shots	rattlesnake shoes	chain gang-like blues: D-Tent Boys: "Dig It Up" rattlesnake wriggling its tail, biting Barf Bag. shoes falling from the sky in slow motion
Stanley on the bus remembering the shoe incident	bus ride through arid, sun-washed desert flashbacks to Stanley's arrest, the court, and pictures from the past	Eels "Eyes Down" point of view changing (Stanley's and bird's eye perspective; aerial shot) voice-over Stanley close-up shots of grandfather, Stanley's posters on the wall in his apartment
Stanley arrives at the camp, is introduced to the guards, inmates, tents, food, camp customs	Mr. Sir: rather old and mean, simple-minded Dr. (!) Pendanski seemingly open-minded and tactful, but insults Zero. Zero sad, obviously an outsider, the other boys mainly concerned with their nicknames; present Stanley with their established pecking order.	Western guitar music close-up of Mr. Sir, appearing stupid and of Stanley being amused by Mr. Sir's name. close-up of Zero
flashback to Clyde Livingston in courtroom	Clyde explains that he cannot understand how somebody could steal from orphans	close-up of Clyde's serious face
flashback to Stanley's grandfather who emphasizes their need for luck	at home at the dinner table	
further flashback to Kissing Kate Barlow	KKB's encounter with Stanley's great-grandfather; KKB steals the treasure chest	close-up of the lipstick mark on his forehead and of the chest with Stanley Yelnats' name plate on it
daily routine in the camp: digging holes – building character series of flashbacks to dirty rotten pig-stealing great-great-grandfather in Latvia	the boys walking to the digging site Mr. Sir, in a rather simple-minded way explains his task to Stanley; other inmates keep "bugging" him by throwing dirt into his hole. Stanley finishes his first hole last; Zero is first great-great-grandfather wants to marry Myra and later emigrates to America Mme Zeroni's advice and curse	Little Axe: "Down to the Valley" close-up of Mr. Sir talking about the camp's philosophy close-up of Stanley's face fading into the features of his great-great grandfather as a young man in Latvia; voice-over: story of great-great-grandfather as told by Stanley's grandfather; several close-ups of Mme Zeroni's face and her fiery eyes; echoing laugh when she speaks the curse; Eastern European violin music; frequent cuts from present to past and back
life, work and recreation in the camp	water distribution Stanley walking back from digging site Mr. Sir frightens Stanley by shooting at yellow-spotted lizards in the dark; boys talk about Mr. Sir	aerial shot showing the vast, moonlike desert extreme close-up of Mr. Sir's bulging eyes repeated gun shots are heard

	Stanley naively shows his fossil to Dr. Pendanski, thinking the Warden might give him the day off; but the Warden is not interested in fossils. Pendanski mentions that the Warden's grandfather owned the lake	special effect: yellow-spotted lizards running after Stanley fade-in to lake as it is today
flashback to the lake, three generations ago	Sam is selling onions as a remedy	instrumental music
recreation at the camp, where a new pecking order is established	boys in recreation room and lining up for water Stanley receives his nickname	
counselling session	Stanley blames his great-great-grandfather for his arrest Zero keeps to himself, but is forced to speak during the counselling session: he affirms that all he likes to do is dig holes.	close-up of Zero's face: Zero's loneliness
flashback to mother writing a letter to Stanley	Stanley answers and Zero asks him to teach him to read and write. Zero is alone even when other boys have fun (dancing)	jazzy hip hop music to which the boys dance
digging and searching	Stanley finds tube, which he has to give up to X-Ray; Stanley tells X-Ray to repart the find on the following day; Warden is informed and drives down to the holes in a vintage; steps out of the car, is visibly pleased, rewards the boys, re-establishes her utmost control over the guards, and has inmates dig on a large scale, even starts digging herself.	Moby: "Honey" close-up of boots close-up of face, later all three guards' faces, Teresa James & The Rhythm Tramps: "I'm Gonna Be a Wheel Someday"
boys on their way back from digging site.	when Stanley is taking a shower he looks for hidden cameras	slow instrumental music
flashback to KKB frequent change of scene from present to past and back boys have to go back to digging individual holes	past: rain is hitting school; Sam and Kate Barlow falling in love; Trout Walker bragging about his father owning the lake; Sam and Kate kiss present: Warden is getting nervous about four days of futile digging on a large scale. past: setting fire to the school; Sam's persecution; Sheriff's abuse; Kate shoots sheriff	same slow, instrumental music Keb Mo: "Just Like You" modern, instrumental music, increasing the tension close-up of sheriff's cheek, with the mark of her lips
digging	sunflower seeds episode; Warden hits Mr. Sir hard in the face.	Pepe Deluxe: "Everybody Pass Me By" close-up of newspaper article about KKB and wanted poster close-up of hand and fingernails
digging flashback to KKB	Mr. Sir's swollen face Mr. Sir takes revenge on Stanley by not giving him any water Stanley begins to understand the connection between their digging and KKB's treasure	close-up of newspaper article, wanted poster and tube with KB on it Stefanie Bentley: "I Will Survive".

reading and writing lessons	Stanley teaches Zero; they start talking about personal things	instrumental music
digging	Stanley and Zigzag fighting Pendanski encourages Stanley to fight back; Warden arrives on the scene; forbids Stanley to teach Zero to read Zero runs away into the desert	Instrumental music (guitar) close-up of Warden's vintage car in the middle of the holes instrumental folk music
Warden and guards talk about deleting Zero's files	Stanley overhears their conversation	instrumental music
boys talking about Zero in the tent	Stanley remembers his grandfather talking about his great-grandfather surviving in the desert for 16 days, saying that he found refuge on God's Thumb	instrumental music
a new inmate, Twitch, arrives in the camp; he talks about how easy it is to steal cars, giving Stanley an idea	Stanley flees, his comrades wave	long shot from Stanley's vantage point showing boys waving to him in the distance. instrumental rock music
Stanley walking in the desert	he sees some yellow-spotted lizards, finds Zero in the boat, where they have "Sploosh" the boys see Big Thumb and walk towards it	several long shots of Stanley walking in the desert Stanley's figure dissolves into donkey cart loud instrumental music when Stanley hugs Zero
the boys start to climb Big Thumb	dangerous climb, steep rocks	Song: Eagle-Eye Cherry: "Don't Give Up" harsh, instrumental music when they are in danger, softer music once they are safe
inmates on their way back from camp talking about Stanley		Western guitar music full shot of group
climbing Big Thumb	Zero is sick and Stanley carries him up the mountain, lays him down in a meadow loud shouts of happiness when they find water and onions; Stanley sings "If only" song; Zero listens	soft instrumental music becoming stronger as Stanley carries Zero up the mountain; Mme Zeroni's voice and loud instrumental music are heard night falls soft instrumental music at night on Big Thumb
cut to the Yelnats' apartment and father's experiments	breakthrough: the old sneaker no longer smells	polka music
boys in onion field flashback to shoe stealing	Zero confesses that he stole Clyde Livingston's sneakers; he was later arrested for stealing a pair of shoes from a store	close-up to Zero's feet; police sirens. close-up of boys' relaxed faces close-up of falling shoes (cf. opening scene)
lawyer arrives at he camp	car approaching; boys talking about Caveman's body; lawyer has dispute with Warden; guards watching through blinds.	full shot of Warden and guards

boys talking on Big Thumb at night flashback to KKB next to Sam's boat now dried-out lake	Stanley and Hector (Zero) share the same feeling; recognition scene; promise: one more hole; Trout threatening Kate, who pronounces the curse: Trout and his offspring will be digging for the treasure for the next hundred years; Kate bitten and killed by a yellow-spotted lizard	Soft instrumental music Slow piano music Picture slowly dissolving into KKB's figure roaming the desert
the boys digging their last hole	they find the hole where the treasure is hidden; Zero sneaks into the camp while Pendanski and Mr. Sir are arguing; Warden aims flashlight at boys, yellow-spotted lizards and treasure; flashback to Warden digging holes with her grandfather; lawyer's car approaching; lizards cover boys' bodies but don't bite	quick violin gypsy music folk rock guitar music close-up of boys' illuminated faces and bodies covered with lizards close-up of Texas number plate long shot of cars approaching extreme close-up of lizards
lawyer arrives with Attorney General	dispute over the treasure; Zero does not give up the chest as he reads Stanley's name printed on it the camps illegal practices are revealed Mr. Sir arrested for carrying weapons thunderstorm and refreshing rain; boys saying goodbye Warden begs Stanley to open the chest car drives off in the rain	alternating close-ups of two women arguing shouts and instrumental music full shot of boys dancing in the rain
chest is opened in the Yelnats' apartment	Stanley promises to share the treasure with Zero (Hector)	
at the bus station	Hector meets his mother and hugs her Stanley tells the end of the story	slow instrumental music voice-over
party in luxurious villa	Sploosh ad on TV party (including Clyde Livingston himself) watch	Songs: Devin Thompson: "Happy Dayz" Dr. John: "Let's Make a Better World"

6.2 Viewing tasks
Before watching the film:
What could the opening shots and the first scenes be?

Draw pictures, write notes for what you want to show at the beginning of the film (the part before the film starts). Choose music that might fit.

sequence of scenes	action, images	camera music special effects
first scene characters objects setting		
second scene characters objects setting		

Now watch the beginning (up to when Stanley arrives at the camp).

● How does it compare with what you imagined?
● In what way is it different?
● How effective is it?

First scene:
The opening shots show a series of images that have almost symbolic value: a rattlesnake rattling its tail, standing for the danger of life in the camp, and a boy stepping on it (Barf Bag who, as Zero reveals to Stanley in the novel, p. 104, committed suicide in this manner) and shoes falling from the sky in slow motion (representing the Yelnats' bad luck – in the wrong place at the wrong time), which hit Stanley on his head, knocking him down.
For students who have not read the book this might be a good start to get interested in the novel itself.

Second scene:
Stanley is on the bus and telling his story as a first-person narrator (voice-over). There are cuts between his bus ride and the flashback to the shoe incident. The inside of the bus is filmed in close-ups, but then the bus and the surrounding desert can be seen in aerial shots from a bird's eye perspective. The vast arid brown landscape filled with lots of crater-like holes offers an impressive picture of the immense extension of the area.
Flashback: The police take Stanley to the Yelnats' crammed apartment, where the grandfather, who obviously lives with the family, criticizes the police and blames everything on the Yelnats family's bad luck. The parents are shocked, appear helpless, while the grandfather asks for a warrant and a lawyer.

Further tasks

Key scenes
Students could be asked to analyze the film language (camera, acting, sound & music etc.) of certain key scenes, i. e. the warden's excited reaction after Stanley has found the tube marked KB, Zero's and Stanley's ' adventure trip to Big Thumb, the scenes following the boys' digging up the treasure chest.

Individual tasks
Watching tasks can be assigned so that individual students or pairs or small groups of students can present their findings after the viewing session. Such assignments could be:

Referring to individual characters:
● Observe how Mr. Sir is presented in the film (age, speech, behavior, movement, postures, clothes, gestures, facial expression).

● Observe how Dr. Pendanski is presented in the film (age, speech, behavior, make-up, clothes, gestures, facial expression).

● Observe how the Warden is presented in the film (age, speech, behaviour, movement, make-up, clothes, gestures, posture, facial expression).
● Observe how Zero is presented in the film (age, build, speech, behavior, gestures, facial expression, relationship to Dr. Pendanski, Stanley, other inmates, his mother).

Referring to character relationships and developments:
● Observe how Kate and Sam are presented in the film (age, speech, behavior, gestures, clothes, props, relationship to other villagers, setting). Compare and contrast Kate's role with other famous outlaws in Western movies like *Cat Ballou*.
● Observe Stanley's behaviour at different stages of the film: a) when he is introduced to the camp; b) his behavior in the camp (attitude to guards, Warden, other inmates); c) teh development of his friendship to Zero; d) his relationship to his family; e) how he relates himself to the memories of the past

Referring to the parallel actions of the past
● Examine how the memories of the past are set off from and connected with the actions of the present (photography, music, transitions …).
● Examine the cinematographic means with which the different levels of the past are set off and combined so that the viewer who has not read the story can follow the storyline

Soundtrack CD
The original soundtrack is available on CD. It contains the following songs:
D-Tent Boys: "Dig It"
Shaggy: "Keep'n It Real"
Eels: "Mighty Fine Blues"
Moby: "Honey"
Teresa James & the Rhythm Tramps: "I'm Gonna Wheel Someday"
Keb Mo: "Just Like You"
Pepe Deluxe: "Everybody Pass Me By"
Stephanie Bentley: "I Will Survive"
North Missippi All Stars: "Shake 'Em On Down"
Eagle-Eye Sherry: "Don't Give Up"
Devin Thompson: "Happy Dayz"
Dr. John: "Let's Make A Better World"
Fiction Plane: "If Only; Eels: Eyes Down"
Little Axe: "Down To The Valley"

7. Additional material

There was an old woman (nursery rhyme)
There was an old woman
Who lived in a shoe,
She had so many children
She didn't know what to do.
She gave them some broth
Without any bread;
She whipped them all soundly
And sent them to bed.

8. Bibliography

Bludau, Michael (1993), *Student's Guide to Better Reading Skills.* Cornelsen: Berlin
Deutsches PISA-Konsortium (2001) (Hrsg.), *PISA 2000.* Leske + Budrich: Opladen
Böge, Friederike (2001), "Böse Kinder in die Wüste". *FAZ* 30.12. 2001
MacKenzie, D. and Souryal, C. (1994), *Multisite Evaluation of Shock Incarceration.* Washington D.C.: National Institute of Justice, U.S. Department of Justice
Peters, M.. et al. (1997), *Boot Camps for Juvenile Offenders Program Summary.* Washington D.C.: Office of Juvenile Justice and Delinquency Prevention, U.S. Department of Justice

Dokumentarfilm. *Bootcamp Jugendstrafvollzug auf amerikanisch.* Pro Sieben 1996, zu beziehen über das Medienzentrum der Region Hannover
Altenbekener Damm 79
30173 Hannover
www.mzrh.de

9. Useful URLs

http://inquiryunlimited.org/lit/poetry/holes.html presents poems related to topics and settings of Sachar's novel
http://www.nmha.org/go/boot-camps evaluates boot camps and offers alternatives
http://voyager.snc.edu/education/s2000middle/holli-michelle/holes/curriculum.html
gives interesting ideas on curriculum connections (fächerübergreifenden Unterricht)
http://www.kidsreads.com/funstuff/trivia/holes-triv1.asp as the site says: offers a *Holes* trivia game
http://www.secondaryenglish.com/holes.html gives an American student's review of the novel
http://library.thinkquest.org/J0113061/ is the site of a unit study based on Sachar's novel; it is highly entertaining and contains numerous quizzes.

Scan chapter 3 one more time and fill in the information you get. (Empty spaces can be filled in later).

	Stanley	**Stanley's father**	**Stanley's great-grandfather**	**Stanley's great-great-grandfather**
full name unusual quality of the name				
place of residence (place where he lives)				
social conditions				
approximate age				
outward appearance (weight)				
profession / job				
character traits				
friends				
pastime activities				

Across

1 The protagonist's surname.
2 His given name
4 X-Ray's skin colour
5 X-Ray's real first name
8 Lewis is ... Bag / Ricky's nickname
13 Squid's real name
14 Zero's first name
15 One of the counsellors is called Mr. ... .
17 For the boys Mr. Pendanski is ... .
18 Magnet's real name
19 One counsellor wants to be addressed as ... Sir.
20 Alan is a ... boy (skin color).
21 Hector's nickname
22 Zigzag's real name
23 Alan's nickname .
24 Stanley is called ... in the camp.

Down

1 Apart from zero , Rex is ..., too.
2 Rex's and Theodore's nicknames
3 Lewis is also called Barf ... .
6 Stanley has the boys' respect, because he is ... .
7 Hector's surname
9 And his nickname
10 José is associated with a ... .
11 The boys all have ... names.
12 Armpit's real name
16 Barf Bag is ... .

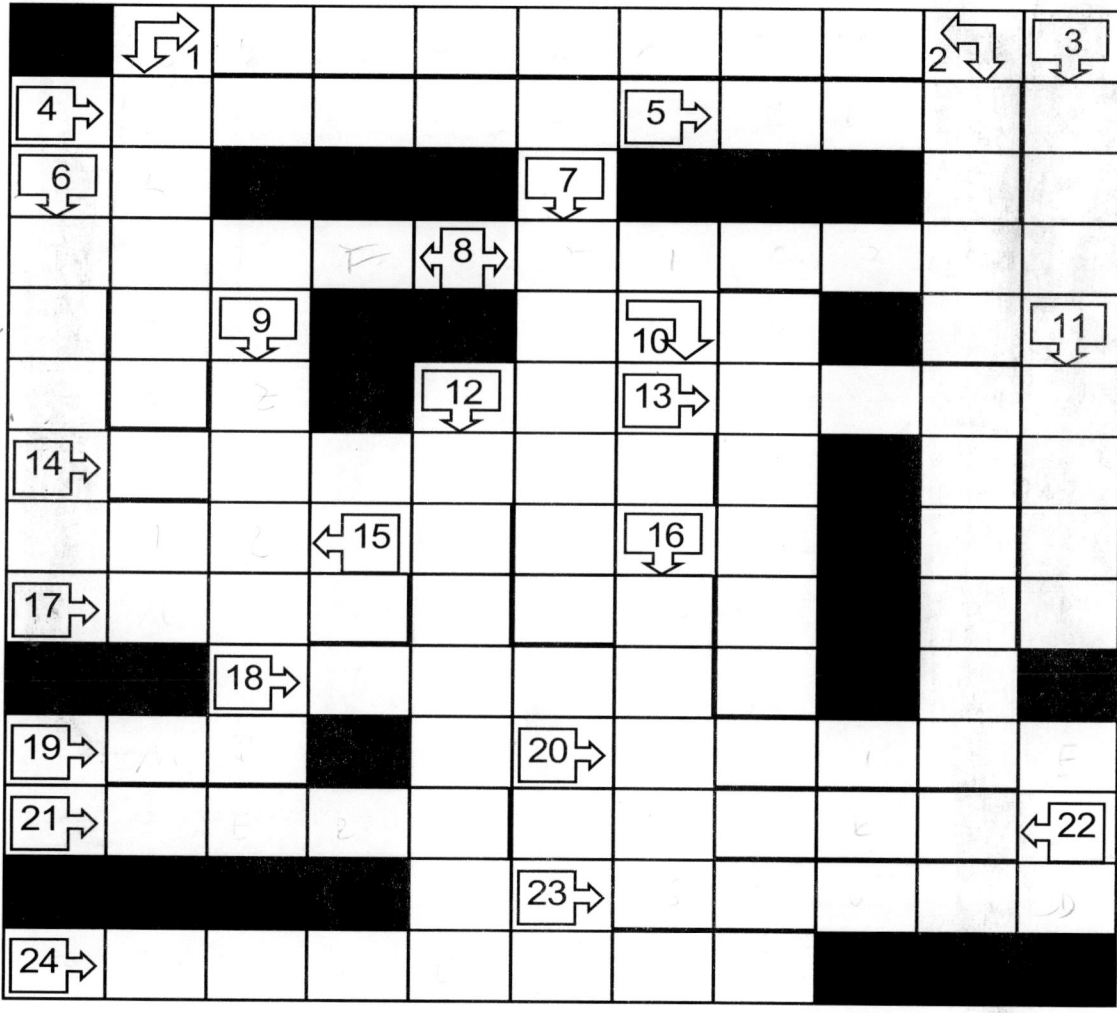

© Ernst Klett Sprachen GmbH, Stuttgart 2003: **Holes** Teacher´s Guide   ISBN 978-3-12-578171-9

Stanley arrives at the camp. After the first 24 hours he sits down on his cot and writes in his diary. Write Stanley's diary entry. It is a mixture of facts about camp life (daily routine, clothes, his tent and the camp's inmates, the area where the camp is situated, the counselor and work) and personal impressions.

Therefore the following task is divided into three steps.

Step 1: After scanning chapters 4 and 5 (pp. 13-19), draw the camp and the inside of a tent as Stanley first sees it when arriving at Camp Green Lake

---

The camp

The inside of a tent

Step 2: Name the objects in your picture.

Step 3: Use the following vocabulary for Stanley's diary entry:
The camp is located in …
a 9-hour bus ride away
It consists of
It is not fenced in
There is / are
Fresh laundry is provided

Adjectives:
blazing – desolate – miserable – run-down – scary – scratchy – smelly – thirsty – vast

 © Ernst Klett Sprachen GmbH, Stuttgart 2003: **Holes** Teacher's Guide   ISBN 978-3-12-578171-9

Step 1 Stanley's criminal record
Stanley had to go to court. The judge sent him to Camp Green Lake. Enter his data into the file that is sent to the camp.
(See chapters 3 and 6.)

Name	Stanley Yelnats
Age	
Place of residence	
Crime	
Criminal record	
Sentence	
Sent to	

The file contains what the authorities probably kept about Stanley. Stanley's view of his "crime", however, is quite different.

Step 2 Write Stanley´s version of his crime.
a. How a narration is done

● Write it as vividly as you can.
● Use details, adjectives and verbs that add color to your story.
● Use direct speech.
● You may even use slang (remember you are writing as Stanley who may be quite angry about a few things).

Therefore the following words may come handy:

to make fun of s.o. – to bully s.o. – bully (n.) – to torment – to curse - bad, worse, worst -
ratio – notebook – to retrieve – to dump – toilet bowl freeway overpass – stinking shoes – to hit – right on the head – a case of bad foot odor –
to drop

incident – sign of God – destiny – bad luck – to believe in fate – ancestor – to run in the family
to blame – patrol car – to arrest – to handcuff s.o. – to question s.o.
to donate – homeless shelter – to sign autographs – to raise money

b. What has to be told

Tell the story of
● how he was made fun of at school.
● what he experienced on the way home.
● his encounter with the police.

And don't forget to add his views on
● his family's bad luck.
● his being in the wrong place at the wrong time.
● his great-great grandfather.

© Ernst Klett Sprachen GmbH, Stuttgart 2003: **Holes** Teacher´s Guide   ISBN 978-3-12-578171-9

Start filling in this worksheet after reading chapter 7. Complete it with the names of Stanley's and Zero's family members whenever you get more information about one of them. Use a pencil so as to make corrections possible.

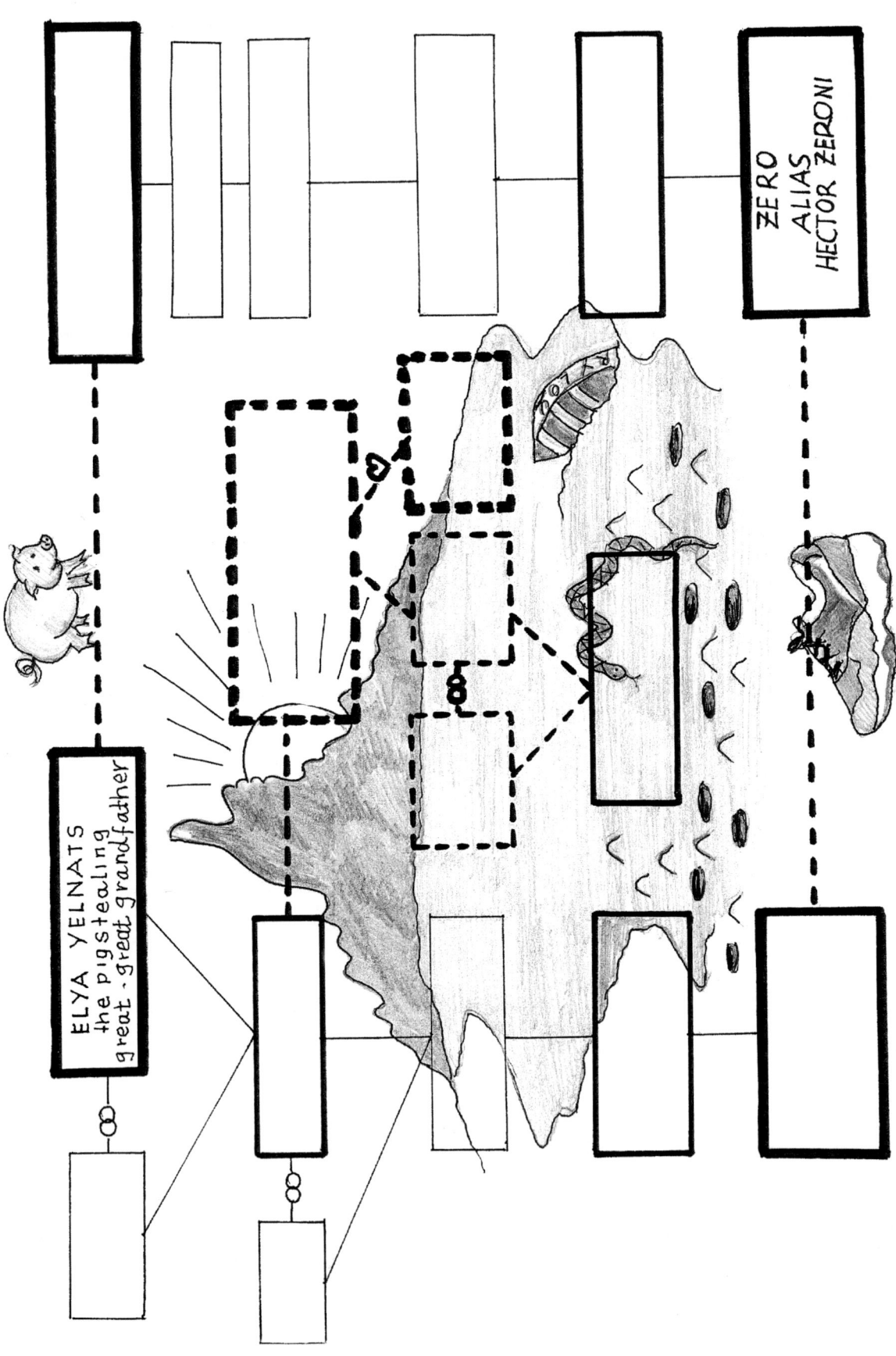

© Ernst Klett Sprachen GmbH, Stuttgart 2003: **Holes** Teacher's Guide   ISBN 978-3-12-578171-9

The guards keep files for every boy. Take Stanley's file as a model and, while reading, update them regularly.

Tent D Name/nickname: Photo	Date of arrival	
	Date of release	
	Crime/misdemeanor	
	Age	
	Skin color	
	Outward appearance	
	Behavior in the camp	
	Other	

Tent D Name/nickname: Photo	Date of arrival	
	Date of release	
	Crime/misdemeanor	
	Age	
	Skin color	
	Outward appearance	
	Behavior in the camp	
	Other	

After reading chapter 22, analyze the character relationships among the boys at the camp. You may use the filled-in files (cf. W6).

Step 1: Find a way to visualize the hierarchy among the boys.

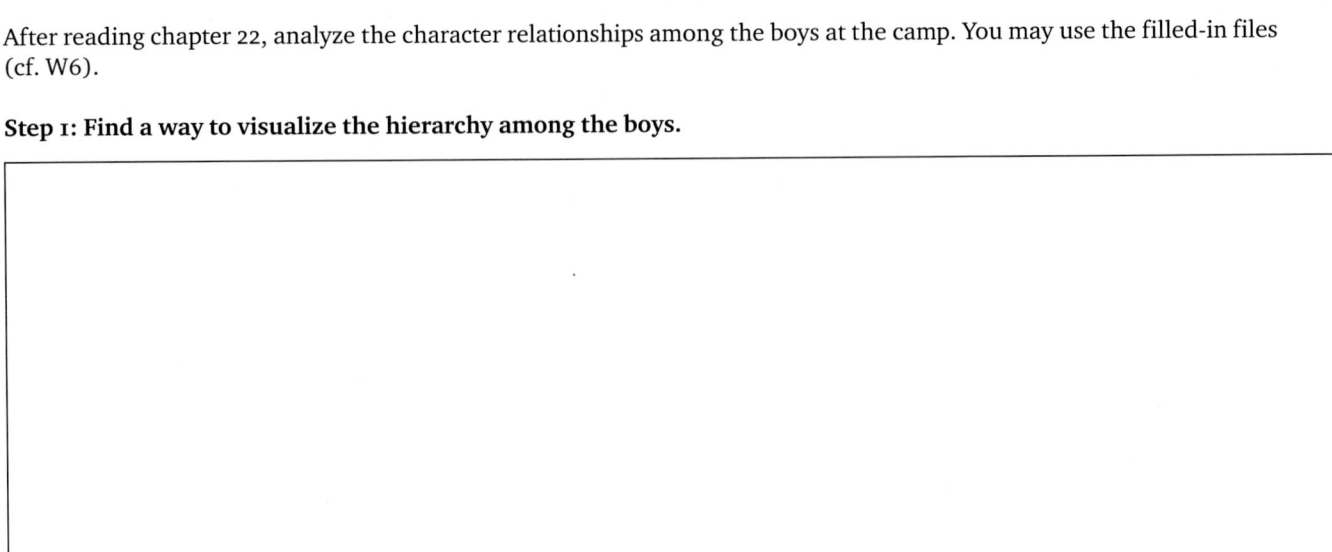

Step 2: Add the roles of each individual to your diagram.
You might want to use words like: ally, boss, bully, clown, to fidget, fighter, loner, loser, nobody, whiner, winner.

Step 3: Analyse the relationship among the boys.
These words may come in handy:

to be clearly defined
it can be compared with
to play an important role
this utterance shows
compared with
according to
concerning
it can be seen in the fact that
so one can say that
this becomes clear when
to come to realize / to realize slowly
to feel / to sense something
this incident shows / explains/
clarifies / mirrors / reflects …

to stick to / obey the rules
the rules set / established by
ritual
to establish one's position
to affirm one's position
to struggle for power and dominance
to be in control of
not to allow any contradiction
to mock at somebody by …ing
to make fun of somebody by …ing
to display power
to run the risk of losing
to experience humiliation
to humiliate
to pretend to
to cope with
to feel inferior to
to defend somebody against
to have the right to
to make sure that / to ensure that
to admit feelings of loneliness and
desperation
to dare to
to appreciate

silent
bearable
acceptable
desperate
lonely
sensitive
envious
curious
determined
introverted
outgoing
dominant
aggressive
clever
dull
intelligent
clumsy

    © Ernst Klett Sprachen GmbH, Stuttgart 2003: **Holes** Teacher's Guide   ISBN 978-3-12-578171-9

Here is the beginning of a diagram that represents the steps of Zero's and Stanley's friendship.

The white space in the middle shows their initial distance. As you read, take notes whenever something is said about their friendship. This diagram with concrete details will later help you to give a report about the development of their friendship (W 17).

If you have another idea of how to visualize the boys' developing relationship, don't hesitate to realize it.

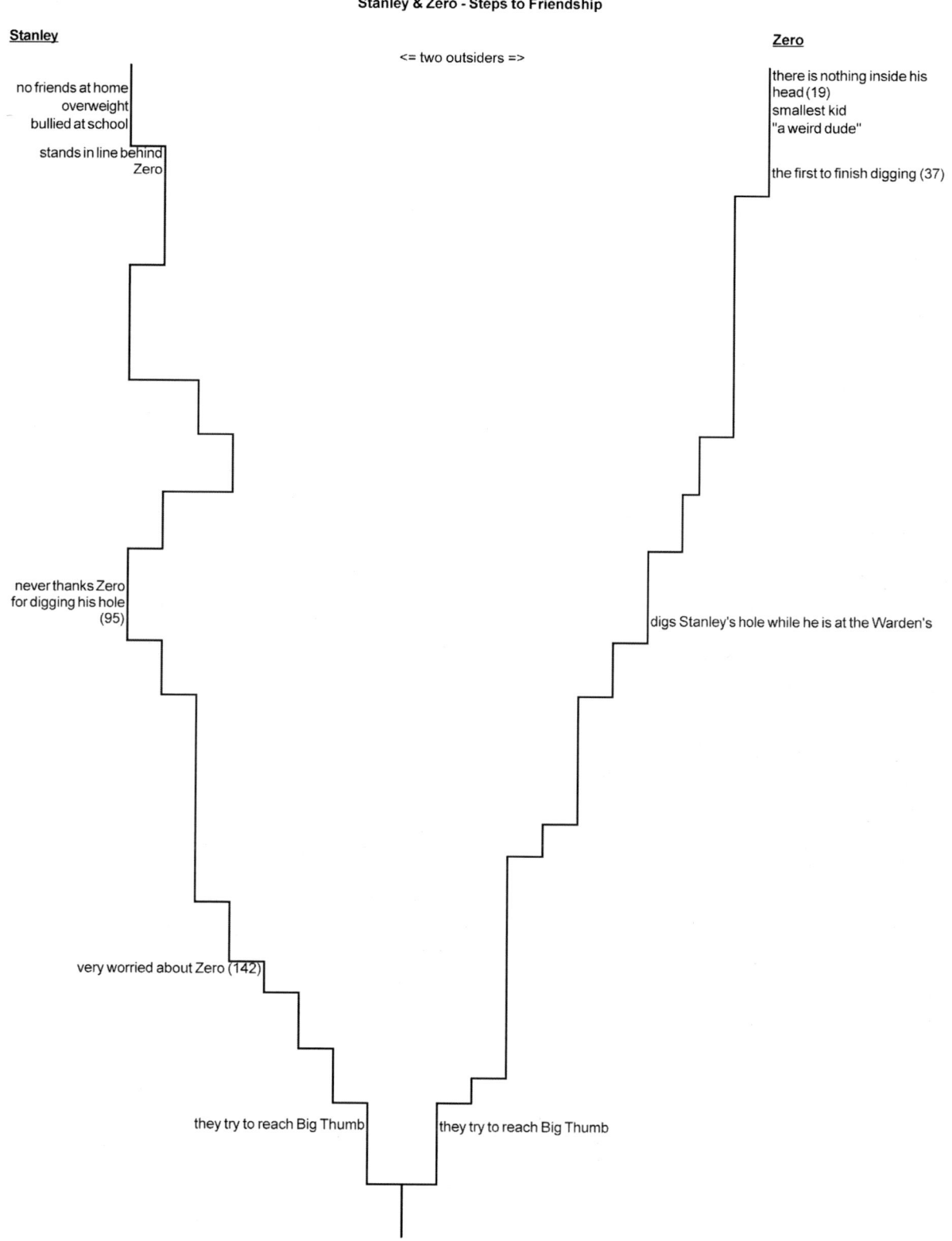

Stanley & Zero - Steps to Friendship

<= two outsiders =>

Stanley
no friends at home
overweight
bullied at school
stands in line behind Zero

never thanks Zero for digging his hole (95)

very worried about Zero (142)

they try to reach Big Thumb

Zero
there is nothing inside his head (19)
smallest kid
"a weird dude"

the first to finish digging (37)

digs Stanley's hole while he is at the Warden's

they try to reach Big Thumb

they become rich and happy

© Ernst Klett Sprachen GmbH, Stuttgart 2003: **Holes** Teacher's Guide   ISBN 978-3-12-578171-9

After chapter 16:
Finish Stanley's letter to his parents (cf. p. 37).
Remember that Stanley does not want to worry his parents and therefore lies about his real life at the camp. Also take a look at his mother's answer on p. 55.

How to write a personal letter:
- date (right hand corner)
- opening (Dear …., Hello …., Hi ….)
- body (separate paragraphs)
- personal questions (i.e. How are you?)
- closing phrase (new line)
- greetings (i.e. say hello to …)
- Love, signature (new line, lower right hand corner)

Dear Mom,

Today was my first day at camp, and I've already made some friends. We've been out on the lake all day, so I'm pretty tired. Once I pass the swimming test I'll get to learn how to water-ski.

Love,
Stanley

© Ernst Klett Sprachen GmbH, Stuttgart 2003: **Holes** Teacher´s Guide   ISBN 978-3-12-578171-9

● **Step 1:** Find the few incorrect statements and put them right.

● **Step 2:** The following events in Kate's life are jumbled up and not in their chronological order. Cut the statements out and put them into the right order. (The following pages will help you: chapter 23 (65f.), chapter 25 (74–77), chapter 28 (82 –84.)

● **Step 3:** Write a complete text about Kate Barlow's story by adding connectives (conjunctions, adverbs, etc. – words like and, or but, for, yet, so, however, either … or, neither … nor, therefore, nevertheless, anyway – look in your grammar for a more complete list) thus logically connecting the facts with each other.

How a historical narration is written:
● chronological order
● new paragraphs for new information
● linking words

List of statements
a) Although there was no telephone in the village the news of Sam kissing Kate spread like wildfire.

b) 110 years ago Green Lake was the largest lake in Texas.

c) Sam was shot and killed in the water and Kate was rescued against her wishes.

d) Trout Walker was one of Ms. Barlow's day-school students.

e) Sam, the onion seller, who often passed the school house, went around with a cart drawn by his donkey Mary Lou.

f) One day Trout invited Kate to a ride in his motor boat, which she refused.

g) Kate came back to Green Lake and lived in an abandoned villa, where she mourned Sam.

h) One day Kate Barlow asked Sam to help her repair the roof of the cow shed.

i) Sam and Kate tried to escape in Sam's boat but were chased by Trout Walker's helicopter.

j) The following morning no kid came to school at all.

k) When Sam said goodbye, Kate hugged Mary Lou's neck, saying that her heart was breaking.

l) Kate enjoyed watching Sam do some odd jobs around the schoolhouse.

m) Then Sam took hold of Kate's hand and kissed her.

n) Kate Barlow, a pretty young woman, lived at the edge of the lake.

o) He cured people of illnesses with his apple juice.

p) 20 years later Green Lake was just a little pond of very clear water.

q) She was the town's only teacher.

r) By the end of the term Sam had turned the old run-down schoolhouse into a little jewel which the whole town was proud of.

s) Sam was not allowed to attend classes because he was a Mexican.

t) Three days after Sam's death Kate shot the sheriff and became an outlaw who robbed all kinds of rich people for the next 20 years.

u) Kate also taught classes in the evenings for adults.

v) Trout Walker and his wife were desperate to get Kate's loot, which she had gathered while being an outlaw, and mistreated her severely.

w) He was a lot more interested in the teacher than in getting an education.

x) Since then not one drop of rain has fallen on Green Lake.

y) Finally a lizard killed Kate, who died laughing, telling Trout and Linda to start digging for the treasure hidden in the ground.

z) The sheriff wanted to hang Onion Sam for kissing a white woman.

1	2	3	4	5	6	7	8	9	10	11	12	13	14	15	16	17	18	19	20	21	22	23	24	25	26

© Ernst Klett Sprachen GmbH, Stuttgart 2003: **Holes** Teacher's Guide   ISBN 978-3-12-578171-9

Create a wanted-poster of Kissin' Kate Barlow. (after chapter 26)

The poster should include
● name
● reward for her capture
● a sketch of the person
● information which could be helpful for her capture

If you are not sure what a wanted-poster could look like, search the internet on the following pages:
www.wildwestweb.net/reward.html
http://tombstoneaz.net/wantedpost.php3?SID=106980501

Here is some room for your first draft:

After chapter 31:

Zero, Stanley's only friend at Camp Green Lake, has run away. Now, Stanley is not only worried about Zero being alone in the desert, he also knows that the Warden, Mr Sir and Mr Pendanski want to erase Zero's file from the computer. This way nobody would ever be asking what happened to Stanley's friend because nobody would know he was at the camp. In addition, the staff of Camp Green Lake would then be able to decide themselves what to do with Zero if he ever returned. They might even decide to kill him.

Stanley feels he has to do something. He thinks about writing to the Attorney-General, he just does not know how to get the letter out of the camp. Maybe he could sneak into Mr Sir's office and break into his computer when everybody is asleep...

Step 1: Note-taking: Description of the staff

Scan chapters 4, 5, 12, 14, 20, 24 and 30 and fill in the chart.

	Mr. Sir	**Mr. Pendanski**	**the Warden**
outward appearance			
nickname			
favourite sentence			
job / position			
habits			
attitude towards the boys			

Step 2: The letter to the Attorney General
Write Stanley's letter to the Attorney General using your notes from the chart.
For the structure of your letter consider the following points:

● Stanley's first encounter with Mr. Sir (Chapter 4)
● Mr. Sir's position in the camp (Chapter 24)

● Stanley's first impression of Mr. Pendanski (Chapter 5)
● Pendanski's function in the camp (Chapter 12)
● How Pendanski changes (Chapter 30)

● The role of the Warden (Chapter 14)
● What the Warden makes of her position (Chapter 20)

How to write a formal letter:
● date (right-hand corner)
● opening (Dear Mr. / Mrs. …)
● body (separate paragraphs)
● closing phrase (e.g. I'm looking forward to receiving your answer)
● Yours sincerely / yours faithfully, signature (new line, lower right-hand corner)

Stanley's letter could start like this. Continue.

```
Dear Mr. Attorney General,

My name is Stanley Yelnats and I am an inmate of Camp Green Lake, a
"juvenile correctional facility", as the sign outside the main office
says. I do not want to complain about our daily duty of digging holes or
that I am here in the first place. I am writing to you, however, to tell
you that I am worried about my friend Zero, who ran away from this place.
I know that it is his own fault if something happens to him out there, but
that is not the reason for my writing. I am even more worried about what
the guards will do to him if he returns. Therefore I will describe the
counselors and the Warden so you can get an impression of them yourself.
First of all, there is Mr. Sir. ...




















I hope you can do something for my friend.

Yours sincerely,
Stanley Yelnats



P.S.: I overheard a conversation in which they decided to erase Zero's
files from the state computers so that nobody will ask any questions. So,
please, act quickly.
```

The camp owners advertise the camp in public and have written a leaflet about the camp which is sent to judges, social workers, the police and other institutions who work with young offenders. Write such an in such an advertisement for your camp. Words and expressions from chapters 4–6 and the list on the right might help you.

You may also want to study advertisements for camps of this sort on the internet, e.g. the homepage of the Turn-About Ranch (www.turnaboutranch.com).

Expressions to help write the brochure:
archeological and wildlife excursions – behavior change – to be located in – to build character – challenging environment – to consist of – correction center – counseling sessions –- fully furnished recreation room – improvement – to keep strict discipline – leisure facilities – to obey authority – to offer orientation – organized free time – to provide fresh laundry – qualified staff – regimented system – regular daily routine – sensitive counseling – sports activities - to turn boys' lives around – to teach respect, discipline, responsibility – time to relax – useful, reliable, hard-working members of society – young offenders

Camp Green Lake

The alternative institution for the improvement of "bad boys"

Most recent research has shown that young people tend to adopt appropriate social behavior more easily when they are in a group of their age under skilful guidance

We offer

We teach

We help

Our motto is

Accommodation (board and lodging)

Equipment

Clothes

Daily schedule

Mornings

Afternoons

Evenings

Slogan

Contact:
CAMP GREEN LAKE
The Warden
Texas 79044
Call toll-free 800 – 831 1269

© Ernst Klett Sprachen GmbH, Stuttgart 2003: **Holes** Teacher´s Guide   ISBN 978-3-12-578171-9

After reading chapter 41:
Two days after carrying Zero up on Big Thumb Stanley lies awake in the night, too excited to fall asleep. He can't remember when he last had these feelings of happiness. A lot of things go through his mind: the miserable time at school, the bullies, his loneliness … He never really accepted himself, but now it's different. He comes to understand why he is so happy now.

Write down the thoughts that might flow through Stanley's mind.
You don't have to follow any rules; just let your mind wander.

After reading chapter 49:

The Story of SPLOOSH

To be a successful inventor you need three things: intelligence, perseverance and just a little bit of luck. Stanley's father does not seem to have any of that, but he remains hopeful nevertheless. While Stanley was at Camp Green Lake, his father was trying to invent a way to recycle old sneakers. Remember, Stanley thought it was a sign of destiny that Clyde "Sweet Feet" Livingston's sneakers fell from the sky. He believed that this might bring about a breakthrough for his father. It turned out that he was right. Stanley did not only meet the person who really stole the sneakers at the camp, he also removed Madame Zeroni's curse from his family by taking Zero up to Big Thumb. Only after the curse had been removed, was Stanley's father able to invent a product which eliminates foot odor.

Now that *Sploosh* has been on the market for a few days, Stanley's father is being interviewed by *Science Today*, a magazine which helped quite a lot of new inventors to become famous. With a partner / group, write an interview with Mr. Yelnats for the next issue of *Science Today*, asking him about the circumstances that led to the invention of *Sploosh*. Also give Mr. Yelnats' answers.

Include the following aspects:
– Mr. Yelnats' motto as an inventor
– hope and destiny (in his family)
– the family curse
– Clyde "Sweet Feet" Livingston's sneakers
– the name *Sploosh*

These words might be useful to you:
to inspire – to invent – a product – to discover – to eliminate – athlete's foot – formula – perseverance – to lack the bit of luck you need to be a success – to remain hopeful – descendant – to break a promise – to be based on – to donate – to be involved

Science Today: Mr Yelnats, what inspired you …

Before reading chapter 50, design an advertisement for *Sploosh* for a magazine or write the script for a TV commercial.

- What should the product look like?
- What should be emphasized?
- What would make a good slogan?
- Who could advertise the product?

Zero and his mother eventually find time to talk about his experiences at Camp Green Lake. Zero tells her how he came to know his best friend Stanley better. In his report he explains to her the difficult beginning and the ups and downs of their friendship.

Take the diagram (W 8) as a basis and highlight those steps in the ups and downs of the friendship which you think important before you actually start to write.

You may find these words and expressions useful:
as if he wanted to – but still – coincidence – to get rid of – humiliating – I couldn't stand being – to be interested in – it is no use fighting – provocation – strange – this is when – to be fed up with – to be caught in a trap – to fall into a trap – to be first (last) in line – to be pleased with – to make a deal – to mention – to react to – to realize – to suggest to s.o. – to tease – unfortunately – weird – what a relief

© Ernst Klett Sprachen GmbH, Stuttgart 2003: **Holes** Teacher's Guide   ISBN 978-3-12-578171-9

"If only, if only," the woodpecker sighs,
"The bark on the tree was just a little bit softer."
While the wolf waits below, hungry and lonely,
He cries to the moo–oo–oon,
"If only, if only."
(pp.11 / 116)

"If only, if only," the woodpecker sighs,
"The bark on the tree was as soft as the skies."
While the wolf waits below, hungry and lonely,
Crying to the moo–oo–oon,
"If only, if only."
(p.33)

If only, if only, the moon speaks no reply;
Reflecting the sun and all that's gone by.
Be strong my weary wolf, turn around boldly.
Fly high, my baby bird,
My angel, my only.
(p.152)

Step 1: Wishes and desires

The woodpecker and the wolf both have a strong wish, which they hope will be fulfilled. The same applies to some of the characters in the book. Consider the wishes / desires and the despair of an individual and fill in the grid.

Stanley	
Stanley's father	
Kate Barlow	
The Warden	
Madame Zeroni	
Zero	

Step 2: Rewrite the song

Focusing on one of these characters and his or her different wishes and / or problems, rewrite the poem / song:

"If only, if only," _____ sighs,

_____

_____

_____

"If only, if only."

Research real boot camps and their effectiveness

There are many websites dealing with boot camps available on the internet; just type in "boot camp" into a search engine and you will find all kinds of information. For those who have no access to the internet, study the following two pages and watch the German documentary *Bootcamp – Jugendstrafvollzug auf amerikanisch* and try to make up your minds on how effective boot camps are. Use the information you get to take a stand in the following panel discussion.

The 20-minute documentary deals with one juvenile correction facility in the U.S.A. It shows the absolutely authoritarian prison-like boot camp which juvenile first-time offenders have chosen themselves in order to avoid a regular three-year prison term. The documentary is an example of how shock treatment and military drill lead to total submissiveness of the 20-some-year-old inmates, who are sujected to constant humiliation. The film claims that the recidivism rate is smaller than the one for regular prison inmates, a figure that is not supported by other statistics (cf. the data of the National Mental Health Association, http://www.nmha.org/go/boot-camps).

Step 1: Add more words to the following list

institution	people	actions / methods	aims
prison	first-time offenders	shock treatment military style training to serve a prison term	to break the inmates' will to shock inmates for life to lower the recidivism rate (Rückfallquote)

Step 2: Write a summary using the words from the above list and the following summary elements.

The documentary deals with ...;
it centers on ...,
it shows, it reflects
the people's behavior is shown in a shocking, interesting way;
life in the camp is described in detail
actions are characterized by ...

How to write a summary:
- introductory sentence providing the reader with a general idea of the topic
- factual style
- logical order
- present tense
- no description
- no personal feelings or opinions

         © Ernst Klett Sprachen GmbH, Stuttgart 2003: **Holes** Teacher's Guide   ISBN 978-3-12-578171-9

Vocabulary

Step 1: To compare and contrast you might need the following vocabulary:

Similarities	Differences
They behave / act similarly in that … / because … They are similar … One similarity is … The … is (almost) the same. Comparing the documentary with the book, I find … Similar to the guards in *Holes* …	They behave / act differently in that they …/ because they … They are different from each other in that the one … One difference, dissimilarity is … The differ from each other The … is totally different. While the guards in the film are always shouting, the guards in *Holes* … In contrast to the guards in *Holes*, …

Step 2: Be aware of how you want to structure a comparison and contrast essay paper:

Step 1: Make an outline of the similarities and differences:	**similarities** 1 2. 3. … **differences** 1. 2. 3. …
Step 2: Topic sentence: Write the most general statement at the beginning:	When I look at the role of the guards in Holes and in the documentary Bootcamp I see a few similarities, but more differences.
Step 3: Decide in which format you want to structure your essay. If you want to analyze the similarities in one go and then look at the differences, you should write at least two different paragraphs. If, however, you compare point by point, several paragraphs will be the result.	 1st paragraph: similarities 2nd paragraph: differences several paragraphs according to number of different points 1st: control 2nd: power and power struggle 3rd: … 4th: …
Step 4: Start with one of the two categories:	Looking at the similarities one can see that both types of guards …; for example, Stanley…
Step 5: Give at least one example of this statement:	Another example of the guards' total control is that …

Situation: The Johnsons have a lot of trouble with their son. He took knives to school, threatened other kids, cut teachers' auto tires and had to be suspended from school several times for unruly behavior. The Johnsons do not know what to do with Jeremy. So they go to a psychiatrist who tells them about a boot camp in Arizona, far away from any living soul. To get more information they watch a TV program on boot camps, which is a 30-minute panel discussion.

In groups of 3–4, design roles for the panel discussion for:

- the moderator (host) of the discussion
- a camp manager
- a camp guard
- a father who sent his son to such a camp and liked it
- a mother who sent her son to such a camp and disliked it
- a youth who has just been released from such a camp
- a judge who opposes boot camps because he has read the Koch Crime Institute report
- a street worker who knows juvenile delinquents from his everyday experience

The audience is invited to participate in the discussion.

How effective are boot camps?

The documentary Bootcamps has given several arguments for boot camps, especially that the recidivism rate is very low. Other arguments for boot camps may be found in a variety of advertisements available on the internet. Below is an article (found at http://www.boot-camps-info.com/bootcamps. html and http://www.boot-camps-info.com/effective.html) that helps you find arguments against boot camps. For further arguments against such camps you may want to have a look at the site of the Friends (= Quaker) Committee on Legislation of California, 926 J Street #707, Sacramento, CA 95814-2707
(http://www.fcla.org/fclLinks.html).

Boot Camps: What Are They?

Boot camps are military-style, semi-penal institutions that use discipline, military exercises, and rigorous physical training to "break" a defiant adolescent and supposedly return home a "good soldier" who will obey authority, follow rules, and improve behavior at home and school.

There is no therapy, no psychological intervention to address underlying emotional or behavioral problems that may have been developing over many years. The theory is that a swift "kick in the pants" will turn around a child who has probably been acting out for years.

There is more than one type of boot camp. Some are state-run substitutes for juvenile jail. Some are privately run "get tough" camps where the "guards" enforce strict rules, some of them simply there for no other reason than to challenge the student to follow the rules or break them, force physical exertion (forced long runs and obstacle courses), and generally shake up the child's perception of reality. Of course, this isn't reality. Most of us do not live in a boot camp or military atmosphere in the real world. These boot camps were created as a short-term alternative to military boarding schools. The idea is that you break the child's will (spirit?) and teach them that they are not the center of the universe.

However, many therapists would disagree that such a tactic results in a well-adjusted, responsible young adult. The recidivism rate of juveniles who attend state-run boot camps has been said to be as high as 94%. That does not say much for the success of this model of rehabilitation.

"Military-style boot camps have been haunted by abusive staff members, even as they were being touted as cheap, effective prison space-savers and politically tasty." *APB News*

"Seven guards from Maryland's boot camps for juvenile offenders have been fired for assaulting delinquents in their care, officials said yesterday as criminal investigations continued into a pattern of abuse spanning more than three years." *Baltimore Sun*, January 11, 2000

"Boot camps use military discipline to try to turn rebellious youngsters' lives around. But over the past decade, as the popularity of such camps has grown, so have abuse allegations, lawsuits and deaths." *Nando Times*, July 6, 2001

Boot Camps: Are They Effective?

Boot camps came into being as an alternative to jail for juvenile delinquents. Research has shown that the recidivism rate for juvenile offenders who have attended a "boot camp" is very high, as high as 90%.

Why would a parent want to send a troubled teen to a program that was originally intended for adolescents who have been prosecuted for criminal acts? It is not an environment intended to modify behavior through self-understanding. It is an environment that seeks to scare kids straight, a method that has proven time and again to have on short-term results.

Whatever program or therapeutic approach you choose for your struggling adolescent should take into consideration the long-term impact of the choice. If a child undergoes significant behavioral and emotional changes in a therapeutic problem, the long-term success rate will be much higher.

Many times parents want a "quick fix" for their troubled teen. How many years did it take to end up with a sullen, belligerent, hostile child? You won't fix it overnight. Focusing on a long-term plan in which the intervention is therapeutic and emphasizes behavioral change through the acceptance of personal responsibility will improve the outlook for your child.

Boot camps are rarely the best choice for a truly troubled teenager. They need to face their basic emotional and behavioral issues as well as discover and be taught behaviors and positive interactions that will improve their academic performance, personal relationships, and personal success. It is change that occurs through self-revelation that has the longest and most permanent effect on any human being. Give your child the opportunity to learn more about himself or herself, and then discover that he or she can be a positive part of the community.

© Ernst Klett Sprachen GmbH, Stuttgart 2003: **Holes** Teacher´s Guide   ISBN 978-3-12-578171-9

Field size
(Bildausschnitt/Bildgröße)

long shot *(Totale)* people/ objects shown from a distance

full shot: shot of the whole body/object

medium shot: upper body /part of an object

close-up *(Nahaufnahme)*: head and shoulders

extreme close-up: *(Detailaufnahme)* face only; detailed shot

Camera movements

static shot: camera does not move

to pan left/right *horizontal schwenken*; to tilt up/down *vertikal schwenken*

crane shot *(Kranfahrt)*: camera moves flexibly in all directions on a crane

to zoom in on/out of s.th. (e.g. a face)

tracking shot *(Kamerafahrt)*: camera is on a vehicle moving on the ground

Camera positions

E.g. A point-of-view shot is seen through a character's eyes. Other examples are:

establishing shot: shows location (long shot/pan) at the start of a scene

overhead shot: bird's eye view

over-the-shoulder shot

reverse-angle shot: from the opposite side, usu. shows a dialogue partner

Camera angles

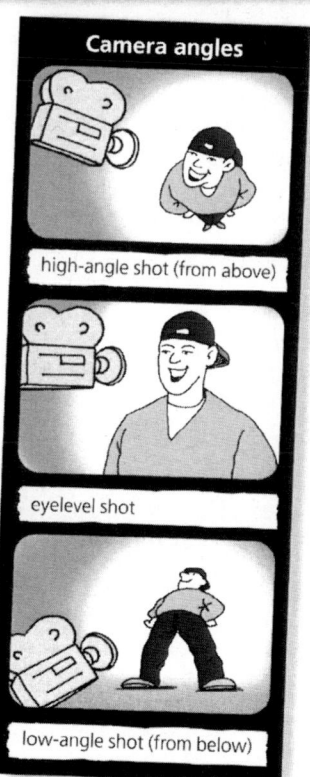

high-angle shot (from above)

eyelevel shot

low-angle shot (from below)

© Ernst Klett Sprachen GmbH, Stuttgart 2003: **Holes** Teacher's Guide   ISBN 978-3-12-578171-9

Student self-assessment

Reading strategies

I now know which reading strategies to use to understand an unknown text

- ☐ infer the meaning of unknown words by looking at word formation
- ☐ asking myself if there are similar words in other languages
- ☐ intelligent guessing from the context or the sounds of some words

- ☐ I can scan texts quickly to find specific information.
- ☐ I can skim texts to find the general idea.

I am familiar with various text types:

- ☐ formal letter
- ☐ informal letter
- ☐ advertisement, commercial, poster
- ☐ distanced description
- ☐ personal description
- ☐ character analysis
- ☐ summary
- ☐ review
- ☐ narration (story)

others:

_____

_____

_____

_____

_____

I can quickly find the purpose of a letter (or other texts); I can tell whether it was written

- ☐ to inform
- ☐ to advertise
- ☐ to complain
- ☐ to ask for information
- ☐ to enquire

I can quickly identify the addressee of a letter (or the intended audience of other texts); I can tell whether it was written to

- ☐ a friend
- ☐ a boss
- ☐ a family member
- ☐ a business partner
- ☐ a young/old audience
- ☐ an educated/less educated person or audience

Writing strategies

I am familiar with some important writing strategies:

I know that it is a good idea to start by

- ☐ taking notes.
- ☐ making a mindmap to collect ideas.
- ☐ structuring the ideas to make an outline.
- ☐ being aware of the audience and the purpose of my writing.

I know that a good text must consist of

- ☐ an introduction (see rules for paragraph building),
- ☐ a main part (mostly consisting of different paragraphs   depending on the logic of the text),
- ☐ a conclusion.

I know that

- ☐ new paragraphs mark new ideas, which are logically connected.
- ☐ a paragraph consists of the topic sentence at the beginning and some text to support this topic sentence.
- ☐ a paragraph should have at least three sentences.

- ☐ that good words and expressions from the novel should be used to improve my writing.
- ☐ that this vocabulary must be collected and applied systematically.
- ☐ that connectives are necessary to make a text coherent.

- ☐ that texts must be revised (at least once) before they are presented.
- ☐ that sometimes a dictionary must be consulted to find better, more suitable, more specific words.
- ☐ that the logic of transitions must be checked.
- ☐ that the logic of paragraphs and the whole paper has to be examined so that the text becomes coherent.
- ☐ that spelling and punctuation must be checked.

I now know how to write various text types such as

- ☐ formal letter
- ☐ informal letter
- ☐ advertisement, commercial, poster
- ☐ distanced description
- ☐ personal description
- ☐ character analysis
- ☐ summary
- ☐ narration (story)
- ☐ review

others:

_____

_____

_____

_____

_____

© Ernst Klett Sprachen GmbH, Stuttgart 2003: **Holes** Teacher's Guide   ISBN 978-3-12-578171-9